Disciples of Christ
in Argentina
1906-1956

DISCIPLES
OF
CHRIST
IN ARGENTINA

1906-1956

By J. Dexter Montgomery

*A History of the First Fifty Years
of Mission Work*

The Bethany Press
St. Louis, Missouri

To Anita

who shared the affection and the friendship of the Argentine people and made our home in their beautiful country more real and meaningful

Foreword

Even without a visit to Argentina, one can appreciate the work done there by the Disciples of Christ. This would be by attending the Park Avenue Christian Church in New York City and meeting four cultured and devout Argentine families who have recently transferred their membership to Park Avenue from the live, progressive Colegiales Church of the Disciples of Christ in Buenos Aires. The head of one family helped to write the educational laws of Argentina and to defend the rights of Protestants; another is an official in the United Nations; another has a business position; and another is doing technical work in a famous New York laboratory.

It is a far cry from churches that are contributing such useful citizens to Argentina and the United States, back to 1914 when I met in Buenos Aires a struggling little group located on the muddiest street I can remember during many wanderings around the world. I had been sent by the Christian Woman's Board of Missions from my work in Mexico to carry a word of cheer to these discouraged workers and to make recommendations concerning a future program. The cabled announcement of my arrival had not been delivered and my only welcome at the port was a tremendous downpour which

7

flooded the flat streets of the great, sprawling city. Before the days of extended pavements, telephones, or taxis, I was told by the cabbie that it was twelve miles out to our Mission, but he would do his best to get me there if I wanted to risk it and if I could dig up eleven dollars. He being the Gaucho type and his motor a big dray horse, we plunged. After some two hours of struggle, the tired animal lay down in a stream we were crossing and would not budge. I trudged on in the dark with two heavy bags until I heard the faint sound of "Praise God from whom all blessings flow." I left my bags under a lonely street light, and, exhausted, stumbled into the meeting house. Recognized by our missionaries, Mr. and Mrs. Tolbert F. Reavis and Miss Zona Smith, I begged off from giving, at the moment, the official message of *cheer* from Indianapolis.

When the rain would allow me to get away from my boarding house, I spent the six weeks of my 1914 visit cheering the discouraged missionaries and discussing detailed plans about enlarging and improving Sunday schools and other activities. I hardly felt the great throbbing life of one of the largest cities in the world and the richest nation in all Latin America. Without a feeling for the great Hispanic civilization, the accomplishments of a proud people like the Argentines, a certain amount of friendship with the nation's educational forces, it was almost like butting one's head against the wall. As already stated, it is a far cry from those early days to the present.

J. D. Montgomery's book reveals how, through new interdenominational cooperation, friendship with the Argentine community, and fellowship with those who were leading the great city in its astonishing development, the earlier circumscribed activities grew into strong churches. The Mission, subsequently, in partnership with the Methodists, built a great Christian school whose graduates were later received without examination in the University of Buenos Aires, and developed a Union Theological Seminary to prepare leaders for the growing Evangelical churches in half a dozen South American republics.

This story of fifty years of sacrificial service comes at a critical time in the history of the largest and richest Spanish-speaking country in the Americas. Because of a benign climate in a solid stretch of nearly a thousand miles of rich, level pampas, the country can produce, more cheaply than any other, great quantities of beef, wheat, and corn which she can exchange for the luxury goods of the manufacturing centers of the world. Probably no other people eat so well and abundantly. But spiritually, the Argentines are not so well off. Their indifference to government, the disdain of reform by a large part of the people, has brought them to their present political crisis. Indifference to religion has long been characteristic of the educated classes and European immigrants. The confidence placed in *Colegio* Ward and its Christian leadership expressed by the fathers and mothers of the thousand students who every year attend its classes, and by the number of educators who visit its campus to study its program, is as significant of Argentina's admiration of Christian character as it is of the success of the Christian mission.

J. Dexter Montgomery here proves himself a good historian. His facts are accurate, his judgments are sound, his illustrations illuminating, and his faith in the power of the gospel is unequivocal. His four years' work in Puerto Rico, eighteen years in Argentina, and the last decade of service with The United Christian Missionary Society in the United States have well equipped him to write such a missionary treatise. The closely packed facts reveal these high lights: reinforcements through interdenominational cooperation, importance of training national leadership, place of lay workers in Protestantism, influence of a Christian school in a big city, legitimate expectations from missionary giving, importance of well-trained missionaries, and ways of identifying foreign workers with local communities.

Having followed intimately the struggles, the defeats, and the triumphs of this first half century of service in Argentina and having personally known most of the fine group of Christian servants, it is a privilege to commend Mr. Montgomery's book to the missionary public, to thank God for the consecrated men and women who have so faithfully served this cause, and to challenge the Disciples of Christ to share more abundantly their faith, hope, and love with the wonderful people of Argentina.

SAMUEL GUY INMAN

Preface

This book tells the story of the first fifty years of missionary work of the Disciples of Christ in Argentina from 1906 to 1956. It is one of a series of histories dealing with the first fifty years of work sponsored by the Disciples in various mission fields. It is the third to appear on the work of the Disciples in Latin America.

The religious body known as the Disciples of Christ is the largest Protestant body to have originated on American soil. In the United States this body is generally designated Christian Churches and in some cases local congregations use the name Church of Christ. In Argentina the term *Discipulos de Cristo* is more generally used. In addition, local congregations are designated Evangelical.

The writing of this book has helped me to relive many of the experiences of the years spent in the Argentine Republic. I am grateful for the privilege of having lived with my family in that great country; for the hospitality of its people; and for the abiding experiences gained there.

I am indebted in the writing of this book to so many people that it would be impossible to mention all of them by name. From my co-workers in the Christian ministry in Argentina I gained many insights and much constructive counsel; from the professors and students of the Union Theological Seminary I received breadth of vision and depth of understanding; and from Christians in the Evangelical churches I shared in the richness of the fellowship of believers.

I am especially indebted to the Disciple missionaries in Argentina for their confidence in asking me to write this history, for reading the manuscript, and for offering invaluable suggestions and additions. Mr. and Mrs. Samuel S. McWilliams and Dr. and Mrs. Paul Andress gave helpful suggestions on the manuscript in its final stages. In addition, Mrs. McWilliams secured valuable data on the field. T. J. Liggett furnished needed photographs from Argentina for use in the book.

Dr. Mae Yoho Ward offered counsel and guidance in the original planning of the chapters and in the development of the manuscript. Miss Genevieve Brown read the manuscript and made valuable comments. J. Edward Moseley edited the manuscript and supervised its publication. My wife, Anna Kate, who shared with me the eighteen years of experience and enrichment in Argentina, has aided me constantly throughout the whole process of preparing the manuscript, giving invaluable assistance with research in locating important data.

For the achievements of the Disciples of Christ in Argentina during this half century recognition must go to the executives who administered the work and guided the planning and the formulation of policy. When the work was opened in 1906 Mrs. Helen E. Moses was president of the Christian Woman's Board of Missions, the sponsoring agency. She was succeeded in 1908 by Mrs. Anna R. Atwater who held the position until The United Christian Missionary Society was founded in 1920. Following this merger she continued as the administrative executive of mission work in Latin America until her resignation in 1926. Miss Lela E. Taylor became associated with the Foreign Division of The United Christian Missionary Society in 1924. Upon the resignation of Mrs. Atwater, Miss Taylor was made executive secretary of the department of Latin American missions in 1926 and she occupied the position until the end of 1939. Dr. Mae Yoho Ward succeeded her and has filled this position since 1941.

Grateful acknowledgment is made to the following publishers for their courtesy in granting permission for the use of quotations from books of which they have the copyright: Abingdon Press, Alfred A. Knopf, Inc., Friendship Press, Harper & Brothers, Macmillan Co., Pan-American Union, The United Christian Missionary Society, and World Dominion Press. Also, to the editors and publishers of the following periodicals and magazines: *The Christian Century, Guia del Hogar, River Plate Reflections,* and *World Call.* To *The Christian Century* and *The Christian-Evangelist* I am grateful for permission to use material which I wrote for those valued journals as staff correspondent while in Argentina.

J. DEXTER MONTGOMERY

Indianapolis, Indiana
December 18, 1955

Contents

PART ONE: HISTORICAL BACKGROUNDS

CHAPTER I

Argentina
in the American Scene

The Republic of Argentina at the eastern southern slope of South America has been constantly
gaining a place for itself in the American family of
nations. Of the twenty-one American republics and
the Dominion of Canada, it is exceeded in territorial size by only three of them, namely Brazil,
the United States, and the Dominion of Canada.
There are also only three of these twenty-two American countries whose population is greater than that
of the Argentine Republic—Brazil, Mexico, and the
United States. Measured in square miles, the land
surface of Argentina is equal to about one-third the
size of the United States. If one thinks comparatively of these figures, Argentina would be equal
in extent to the twenty-five states east of the Mississippi River, including the District of Columbia,
and still there would be ample room within Argentina to place the present Republic of France. Were
comparisons made with European countries, Argentina is equal to the combined areas of France, Germany, Italy, the United Kingdom, Ireland, Belgium,
the Netherlands, Austria, Spain, Portugal, Switzerland, Denmark, Poland and Lithuania, and would
still leave room for the inclusion of Jamaica, Puerto
Rico, and Hawaii.

Great plains in Argentina offer fertile fields for wheat, corn, flax, cotton, sugar, tobacco, fruits, vineyards, and grazing. "It has been estimated that if all her arable land were properly cultivated Argentina alone could support a population of a hundred million and, at the same time, export foodstuffs for an equal number outside."[1]

The period from 1906 to 1956, which is the half century since the Disciples of Christ began work in the Republic, shows remarkable progress in the history of the country. The population of Argentina in 1909 was estimated at 6,805,684,[2] while (forty-four years later), according to a United Nations estimate in 1953, there were 18,379,000 inhabitants,[3] an increase of 150 per cent. Should this same rate of increase continue for another fifty years the population of the Republic would reach some 33,560,000 by the end of this century.

The capital city of Buenos Aires with a population of 3,600,351 is the largest city south of the equator and the second largest Latin city in the world. Also, it occupies the unique place of being the third largest city in the two Americas, being exceeded in the number of inhabitants only by the cities of New York and Chicago.[4] About one-fifth of the entire population of the Republic live in the capital city of Buenos Aires. This beautiful, modern metropolis is a growing city. It has torn down

[1]Webster E. Browning, *The River Plate Republics* (London: World Dominion Press, 1928), p. 27. Used by permission.

[2]Samuel Guy Inman, "Argentina," *The Encyclopedia Americana* (30 vols.; New York: Americana Corporation, 1953), II, 197.

[3]"Argentina," *The World Almanac 1955 and Book of Facts* (New York: New York World-Telegram and The Sun, 1955), p. 334.

[4]*U.S. News & World Report*, July 1, 1955, estimated the population of Greater Buenos Aires at 5,000,000.

houses to make the widest boulevard in the world.
It has an underground parking lot for 3,000 cars.
Its people are like their North American neighbors,
for they boast of having the biggest and best of
this and that. They are devotees of good food and
better steaks cannot be found than those served in
the restaurants of Buenos Aires. In addition to
streetcars and city buses there are five subways
to care for transportation within the city and its
suburbs while seven railway systems connect the
capital city with other parts of the nation and with
the neighbor republics. A large and commodious
harbor on the River Plate and a large airport bring
the city into contact with the outside world. The
airport *Ministro Pistarini,* located nineteen miles
from Buenos Aires, is one of the world's largest
air terminals. Visitors to this cosmopolitan city
are impressed by its wide avenues, modernistic
architecture, lovely parks, gorgeous theaters, many
bookstores, educational centers, and bustling commercial life. Just to walk down the Calle Florida,
which each late afternoon is closed to all wheeled
traffic, is an adventure in world outlook, for prac-
tically anything that can be bought in the world can
be purchased there.

In recent years the Republic of Argentina has
been rapidly transformed from a rural to an urban
economy. Today within the country as a whole,
about two-thirds of the population live in cities of
100,000 or more. This change is seen in its truer
character as one views it in a longer perspective.
During the hundred years from the mid-nineteenth

to the mid-twentieth centuries, Argentina's economic life has been revolutionized from a simple pastoral economy to its present highly diversified and regulated state. At the turn of the half-century in 1950 industrial output in Argentina ". . . accounts for roughly one-half of the total national production, as compared with 40 per cent contributed by agriculture and livestock. This is perhaps the most significant index of the radical changes which have taken place in the Argentine economy, still regarded by many as basically agrarian."[5]

Argentina became a Federal Republic with a constitution, adopted in 1853, very closely modeled upon that of the United States of America. It is composed of seventeen provinces, six territories, one federal district and one military district. The legislative power is vested in a Congress of two houses, a Senate and a Chamber of Deputies. The Senators and the Deputies are elected for a term of nine years by a direct popular vote of the people. The President and Vice-President are elected for a term of six years. Prior to 1949 they could not be re-elected, but changes in the constitution were passed in that year which now make it possible for them to succeed themselves in office by re-election. The President and Vice-President are elected directly by a plurality of votes with all parts of the country forming a single district. Before the constitutional reforms of 1949 they were chosen indirectly by electors representing the provinces, Federal Capital, and the national territories. The

[5]*Argentina* (Washington, D. C.: Pan-American Union, 1952), p. 23.

President and the Vice-President must profess the Roman Catholic faith.[6]

Argentina holds high standards in education with a well-planned public school system and a capable group of teachers who are graduates of their carefully planned normal schools or universities. In general the Provincial Governments are responsible for primary education, and the Federal Government for secondary. The schools in the federal district and in the six territories are under the jurisdiction of the Ministry of Education. Primary education is compulsory up to the age of fourteen although it is doubtful that there are schools available to accommodate all the children of school age.

Some who read this book may wonder how the people of Argentina feel toward the United States. So the views of an Argentine, George P. Howard, who is a good friend of his North American neighbors, are quoted on this topic:

In all these countries [Latin American] there is a spirit of good will and friendliness toward their big North American brother. But there are also those to whose interest it is to foment ill will toward the United States. In spite of much that has been said of Argentine antipathy to the United States, you will find in Buenos Aires a public school that carries the name of the United States of North America. As you enter the hall you will see a bust of Washington and one of Lincoln, and by the side of the soft blue, white, and blue of the Argentine flag is the red, white, and blue of Old Glory.[7]

---

[6]By action of the Federal Congress in 1955 steps were taken to modify this requirement.

[7]*We Americans: North and South* (New York: Friendship Press, 1951), p. 6. Used by permission.

Chapter II

Religious and Cultural Backgrounds

The elements entering into the social heritage and culture of Argentina are highly complex. Along with the educational and religious are the political, the economic, and the social institutions. These all become phases of the various departments of human interest which are interwoven in such an intricate way that the culture is all of a piece; the economic supports the political; the political undergirds the religious; the religious buttresses social distinctions.

Argentina, in a significant way, is passing through a profound crisis which affects all of the elements in its culture. This crisis has been in process for a generation and is an episode in the historical development of the nation. Argentina is a comparatively new country and has not reached the stage of mature democracy as have some other western countries, such as the United States of America. But the Argentines have had traditional elements of liberalism and democracy since the middle of the nineteenth century and these elements have been strengthened in recent decades. Even though the crisis has slowed up the process, the essential greatness of Argentina is unimpaired. There is apparently no great danger from the left, because communism has no hold in the Army, it has little in-

fluence in the labor unions, and has no wide ac-
ceptance among the students in the universities. It
presents no great intellectual appeal to the Argentine people. One of the strongest Argentine char-
acteristics is a sense of national dignity and a profound belief in the future greatness of the country. The people have a strong feeling for the country's good name and prestige. Having spent some
eighteen years in Argentina, I believe that this
country will become an effective democracy because
of latent powers which have been shaping up in its
people for a century.

This chapter summarizes some important developments during the years immediately preceding the
opening of the work of the Disciples of Christ in
Argentina, as well as during the fifty years of Disciple work in that republic. As one endeavors to
interpret dominant trends in the Argentine culture
with its ingredients of economic, religious, political, and social customs and practices, certain basic
facts must be kept in mind. The Argentine people
are cosmopolitan in outlook. Argentina and Uruguay are the two most European countries in all of
Latin America. Argentina lies almost wholly in
the south temperate zone with an invigorating climate which is reflected in the outlook of its people.

As the twentieth century opened, the government
of Argentina was conservative but stable. During
the second decade a liberal regime came into power
which continued with success for some two decades,
when the trend was again back toward a conservative government. Also, during the early part of
the century, under the conservative government,

there was, in many respects, more freedom for the Protestant churches to promote and carry forward their work than was the case fifty years later. In the same way liberty of thought and freedom of speech became more restricted as the government changed from its liberal position in the second and third decades to another conservative government.

The religious development of Argentina was not different from that in its neighboring republics. The whole South American continent was isolated from the great currents of religious reform that swept over Europe following the Protestant Reformation and which were eventually carried to North America, but did not reach to any comparable extent the southern continent. Even the Catholic revival, a reaction that took place early in the nineteenth century, scarcely affected the Roman Catholic Church in Latin America. At best, in its spirit and organization, Roman Catholicism as it existed in Latin America at the end of the nineteenth century was still strikingly similar to what it was in Spain and Portugal in the sixteenth and seventeenth centuries, except as it had been brought into contact with the Evangelical[1] movement.

The Roman Catholic Church found it difficult to maintain its work in an effective way in these far distant fields, particularly following the struggle for political independence in the Latin American countries. One difficulty which arose was the transfer of the administrative relations of religious func-

---

[1]"Evangelical" is used throughout this book as equivalent to "Protestant," in accordance with Latin American usage.

tions which previous to the political independence of the colonies had been delegated by the church to the kings of Spain. When the colonies broke from Spain and set up their respective governments the relationship with the church at Rome was also interrupted. Some years elapsed before this relationship again functioned normally. Issues involved are indicated by the close alliance between the religious and the political powers. ''The church and the government became a single entity. The church councils became civic assemblies. The religious perception lost its intimacy in order to become a social norm.''[2] Many factors, including social, economic, and political, contributed to the complexity of the problem and by the close of the nineteenth century large segments of the population had fallen away from the dominant church, including many of the upper classes as well as of the masses. The church did not possess sufficient vitality to recruit the number of priests from its indigenous constituency to give adequate pastoral care to its nominal children. This left many without the normal ministries of the church and without proper religious teaching. Ignorance prevailed among the masses and deplorable distortions of the faith resulted.

With this estrangement between the teaching of the Roman Catholic Church and large groups of the populace in Argentina, the field was ripe during the closing decades of the nineteenth and the opening years of the twentieth centuries for new cults as well as the materialistic philosophy of certain Eu-

[2]Juan B. Teran, *El Nacimiento de la America Espanola* (Tucuman, Argentina: Miguel Violetto y Compania, 1927), p. 184.

ropean leaders to take root in Argentina. This materialistic philosophy, particularly that taught by Comte and Hebert Spencer, won many followers among the intellectuals.

The influence of this materialistic philosophy had become so effective in Argentina and neighbor republics by the opening of the twentieth century, that the intellectual class was found to be almost entirely outside of the church. This opposition or indifference to the church was not so much anti-religious as it was anti-clerical. Intellectuals, in large measure, broke with theological concepts of the day by placing the emphasis on humanity as the supreme object of devotion. The inherent idea in this philosophy made humanity ". . . the new centre of unity and the religion of humanity with its golden rule of love the link uniting all nations . . ."[3] This appealed to a people who pride themselves on being universalists and at the same time gave them a certain smug feeling of superiority. It took away any appearance of religious sectarianism and made them the ". . . heirs of all human and religious values. . . ."[4]

Thus the emphasis on scientific investigation as over against religious truth, made itself felt on the ethical and moral life. The trend was to break away from established standards of conduct and to undermine accepted rules of behavior. It broke away from the old inhibitions based on superstition

---

[3]John A. Mackay, *The Other Spanish Christ* (New York: Macmillan, 1933), p. 168. Used by permission.
[4]*Ibid.,* p. 169.

and fear of future punishment, and replaced them by freedom of thought and the supremacy of natural desire. This change manifested itself both in personal morals by the satisfaction of natural impulses, and in the social ethic by the materialistic application of the theory of the survival of the fittest. Its influence has been great and, in large measure, held sway among many circles in South America until the third decade of the twentieth century. An Argentine, writing in this decade, states the dilemma in somewhat the following way: that moral greatness without the guidance of knowledge may lead to fanaticism, but that knowledge, learning, and science if it is not supported by moral greatness may result in skepticism which is suicide, denying the existence of love which is the soul of the world.[5]

Other segments of the population were also lost to the dominant church. The less educated classes in Argentina became fertile fields for new doctrines. Among these groups theosophy and spiritualism gained adherence in large numbers at the close of the nineteenth century and during the early years of the twentieth century. As summarized by one student in the field:

. . . Perhaps it is to be expected that when an awakened spiritual hunger begins to show itself after a hundred years of bleak materialism, it should desire, not so much a return to organization and ritual and ecclesiastical form, but rather a loose, expansive creed which accepts truths from all religions and guarantees that there shall be no heresy hunts.[6]

[5]Juan B. Teran, *La Salud de la America Espanola* (Paris: Casa Editorial Franco-Ibero-Americana, 1926), p. 106.
[6]Samuel Guy Inman, *Latin America, Its Place in World Life*. Used by permission of Harper & Brothers, Publishers.

These yearnings for a more vital spiritual experience were the forerunners perhaps of a definite turn in the religious thinking of the Argentine people during the second quarter of the twentieth century. Several developments following 1925 indicated specific ways that this search for a fuller religious life was evident in the thinking of the Argentine people. One development was the recognition shown persons from outside the country who brought messages of a spiritual character or messages that were distinctly Christian. Among such speakers were the Hindu philosopher Jinarajadasa who lectured to great audiences in the larger cities on theosophy; and E. Stanley Jones, the widely known missionary to India, who preached to packed houses during a visit to Argentina.

Writings of leading Argentine scholars were another evidence of this development. Dr. Ricardo Rojas, formerly president of the University of Buenos Aires and one of the most conspicuous historians and men of letters in Latin America at the time, published his book entitled *El Cristo Invisible* in 1927. An English edition was published in New York in 1931 under the title *The Invisible Christ*. The book is written as a series of three dialogues between the author and a Roman Catholic bishop. The writer sets forth his endeavor to understand the Gospels as an inspiration of life. His thesis reveals the conflict of religious ideals as well as symbolizes the deep yearning of the Latin-American spirit. Through the dialogue the writer affirms that he is a Christian, both by lineage and by sentiment, although he does not classify himself as either a

Catholic or a Protestant. He states clearly and succinctly his belief in the following passage:

Today I find my surest spiritual guide in the *Gospels*. All sacred books, and the history that chains them together, and the philosophy that explains them, are reading which, far from being pernicious, helps me to understand the profound meaning, always more human and more luminous, of the Christian message. Now I understand why the Lord said that man shall not live by bread alone, but by every word that proceedeth out of the mouth of God, and when I hear the Master of Man speak, the contradictions of fanaticism calmly fade away in the light of his truth.[7]

This religious truth, continues the author, to become effective, must go beyond institutions and organizations and touch the conscience of individuals, becoming a force in their lives

. . . and victory will be on the side of evil, that is to say, of passions, instinct and brute force, if the various religions continue crystallized in rituals that lack spiritual life, and if all civil institutions, like the press, the theater, the school, the factory, and the state itself, forget that it is their duty to care for souls, that they have a mission of fraternity on earth and justice among men.

. . . .

. . . When Christ becomes a reality in the conscience of each man . . . his Spirit will transcend to thought, to custom, and to institutions.[8]

The Roman Catholic Church also contributed in turning the trend back to religious influences. Its leaders were aware of the religious conditions in these countries and had earlier set in motion plans to remedy them. Responsibility had been placed upon orders and organizations within that church to work toward this end. Results of this effort were seen early in the twentieth century. Kenneth S.

[7]*The Invisible Christ*, by Ricard Rojas. Translated by Webster E. Browning (New York: Abingdon Press, 1931), p. 296. Used by permission.

[8]*Ibid.*, p. 299.

Latourette appraises the results of this effort in the following way:

> Rome and the Roman Catholics of Europe did not supinely accept the grim condition of their Church in Latin America. They sought to come to the rescue. Partly as a result, by the year 1914 the Church registered some improvement. It reached its low point in the first half of the century and thereafter achieved gains.[9]

A part of this growing emphasis of religion was the creation by the Roman Catholic Church in Argentina in the early 1930's of a number of new bishoprics and archbishoprics. Perhaps the greatest single historical occurrence which showed this deeper concern for religion was the holding of the 1934 International Eucharistic Congress in Buenos Aires. Outstanding speakers and leaders of the Roman Catholic Church were there from all parts of the world. The Apostolic delegate at this Congress later became Pope Pius XII.

Another source of the new religious awakening which emerged in Argentina, was the Evangelical movement which has been creative and has made its impact through the simplicity of its teaching and the sincerity of its message. Its contribution has been made in a variety of ways. The hearts of believers have been moved when the humble colporteur distributed a copy of the New Testament; when a pastor has set forth the Sermon on the Mount, related the message of some of the beautiful parables, or preached the good news of the gospel. In the same way the religious awakening has been enhanced when a teacher in a school has introduced

---

[9] *A History of Christianity* (New York: Harper & Brothers, 1953), p. 1288. Used by permission.

a new system of mental tests; when a Y.M.C.A. secretary has organized a new program of athletics; or when an outstanding lecturer has presented the principles of the Christian faith. These are all elements of the continuous process of constructive, creative contributions to the religious awakening which has been made by the Evangelical churches.

Mission schools penetrated into new fields through their educational program. In addition to exercising an influence in the formation of character in their alumni, they set standards of educational efficiency and ethical idealism. This educational program also includes the literature produced by the Evangelical forces for use in churches, schools, and homes. This has been done through the translation of literature from other languages and increasingly by the production of literature written by Argentine authors who have taken their place among the leaders of the Evangelical movement.

Turning now from the religious thought of the Argentine people, consideration will be given to political trends during the second quarter of the twentieth century. The following words of Germán Arciniegas, a Roman Catholic and a native of the Republic of Colombia, may help the reader to see the picture in its larger perspective:

There are two Latin Americas, one visible and official, the other invisible and unofficial. In those countries in which the representative system of government has been done away with, the visible reflects a temporary situation resting on violence and favored by fortuitous circumstances. Invisible Latin America is the liberal spirit that lives on in the suppressed majorities.[10]

[10]*The State of Latin America* (New York: Alfred A. Knopf, Inc., 1952), p. 15. Used by permission.

In the struggle for democracy and freedom in the Argentine Republic, 1930 marked the beginning of significant developments. For a half century previous to that date the efforts on the part of liberal leaders to establish a democratic government in the republic made steady progress. The two administrations previous to 1928 were particularly characterized by their democratic ideals and their allegiance to the Argentine constitution. Following 1930, a conservative government began a trend which led to the dictatorship of President Juan D. Perón. Something of a democratic government continued after 1930, but only at times was democracy restored to Argentina. Following the revolution in 1943 the trend toward dictatorship was more and more marked.

The revolution which overthrew the Irigoyen government in 1930 revealed a struggle at the same time political, economic, social, and religious. Following World War I large numbers of immigrants went to Argentina from southern European countries and from the Near East. This influx added greatly to the middle, professional, and skilled working classes. Along with this tide of immigrants, there was growing the idea of democracy among the populace of Argentina. One phase of the struggle which ensued was between this democratic element and the landed aristocracy, the latter having controlled the government in Argentina almost without exception previous to the overthrow of the government in 1930. The tension between the democratic concept and the conservative concept as held by the landed aristocracy was one of the contributing factors to the prolonged revolutionary government following the overthrow of President Hipolito Irigoyen.

The economic depression of the 1930's was keenly felt in Argentina as elsewhere and contributed to the political instability in the country.

World War II played a part in determining the character of government, particularly after 1943. The military government which came into power favored the Nazi and Fascist powers. The attitude of young Argentine officers is not hard to understand in the light of the fact that since the early 1900's the Argentine Army had been trained by German instructors. Later, many of the leading army officers went to Germany and/or Italy for study and there were indoctrinated in the military ideals of those countries.

Another factor of importance which contributed to the rise of *Peronismo*[11] was the change in the nature of the Argentine urban working class. This class had become more Argentine in loyalties in view of the fact that following the depression immigration came to a virtual standstill and sons of former immigrants were now taking the place of their fathers as laborers. Also, there had been a sizable migration from the rural sections of Argentina into the larger cities during the depression and following World War II. This change in the nature of the working class made it easier for Perón

[11]*Peronismo* is the term used to designate the movement which Juan D. Perón headed and which led to his election as president of Argentina in 1946. This implies also the significant place this movement gave to the laboring classes and their influences in government. *Peronista* party is the official name given to the political party which came into being under the first administration of Perón and it was under this party that he was elected to a second term in 1952.

to win them into his labor movement as a larger
per cent of the workers were now Argentina citizens.

Along with this trend in national loyalties was
the rising self-consciousness of the underprivileged
in Argentina, to which group many of the laboring
class belonged. President Perón, with the support of his wife, gave recognition to and made a
place for this group of Argentine citizens. A knowledge of the circumstances which brought this about
helps one to a better understanding of *Peronismo*.
Eva Perón, more than her husband, shared in the
hardships of the underprivileged workers and was
able to identify herself with them. In her book,
La Razon de Mi Vida (The Reason of My Life),
she expressed clearly the sentiment of the op-
pressed, which from childhood was the driving force
in her life. She not only understood the hardships
of the poor, but was inclined to blame the rich for
their poverty. This ability to comprehend the
underprivileged is one of the significant factors
which contributed to the success of the *Peronista*
party. The understanding of these factors helps
one to appreciate the unique place occupied by the
laboring class in Argentina under the administration of Juan D. Perón.

Yet another element which helped advance the
labor movement was the fact that in the preceding
twenty years or more no government had taken any
interest in the trade union movement in particular
and in the working class in general. While it is true
that Hipolito Irigoyen, President of Argentina, had
been pro-labor during his first term, the govern-

ments thereafter took but little interest in labor's needs and wishes.

As one follows the political developments subsequent to the overthrow of the government under President Irigoyen in 1930, it is well to keep in mind that Juan D. Perón headed the troops who entered the Capital and forced the government into submission.[12] Although Perón did not came into public prominence until after the second revolution thirteen years later, he soon rose in influence and power.

In keeping with the tendency toward authoritative government following this revolutionary period, a closer alliance between church and state developed. This in itself was perhaps a normal consequence, since Roman Catholicism was the state religion. However, significant developments took place as a result of this growing alliance.

A law passed in 1884 had established that education in the state-supported schools would be secular. This meant that although Catholic schools would not be forbidden, there would be no teaching of religion in the public schools supported and conducted by the government. In succeeding decades the issue of lay education in the public schools was hardly a serious factor in Argentine politics.

A change came about, however, when during the 1940's an alliance was reached between the *Peronista* government and the Catholic hierarchy in Argentina. This resulted in a reversal of the law which had been in effect for more than a half century.

----

[12]Arciniegas, *op. cit.*, p. 50.

The crux of the above-mentioned alliance seems to have been the re-establishment of compulsory Catholic religious instruction in government schools. This was brought about in 1946 when the Bureau of Religious Education was set up in the Ministry of Education. Widespread opposition was manifest on the part of teachers, non-party educators and political figures as well as certain other political parties. But this was of no avail and approval was later given to this educational measure by the *Peronista*-controlled Congress. This general attitude of the government was reflected in its endorsement of other activities of the Roman Church.

As an example of the attitude on the part of the government during this era, in contrast with previous regimes, religious parades were allowed to take place through the streets of Buenos Aires during Easter Week. Such demonstrations had been virtually unknown in Argentina—at least in Buenos Aires—before the fifth decade of the present century.

This trend toward closer alliance continued to grow and received outspoken support by church officials as well as government leaders. One outstanding exception was that of Monseignor de Andrea[13] who strongly opposed the attempts of the government to gain control of the trade unions. He was also forthright in his defense of freedom of speech, the press, democracy, trade union autonomy, Christianity, and the Argentine constitution.

The results of this alliance between the Argentine government and the Roman Catholic hierarchy

[13]Monseignor de Andrea was a Bishop of the Catholic Church and well known for his liberal views, forthright support of civil liberties, social justice, and fair dealing for the underprivileged.

on the Protestant movement was felt in many ways.
Not only were there restrictions on public preaching and publicity, but for certain periods the use
of the radio by Protestants for broadcasting pur-
poses was suppressed. As regards the teaching of
religion in Protestant schools, much anxiety was experienced. However, more consideration was shown
than strict enforcement of the government decrees
would have permitted. Further consideration of
the limitations placed on Protestant churches will
be included in the body of this history.

While this understanding between the church
hierarchy and the government resulted in much of
the old anti-clerical feeling dying away, there was
considerable dispute as to its long-run value for the
church. Certainly it became evident during the administration of President Perón that the relations
between the *Peronistas* and the Catholic Church
cooled noticeably. Several clashes between the two
tended to weaken the bonds that united them. Perhaps one of the underlying causes of the cleavage
was that regarding teaching in the public schools.
The government not only reintroduced Catholic
teaching in state-supported schools, but also introduced systematic teaching as to the *Peronista* party
among the school children. Teachers were required
to devote time during the school day to the discus-
sion of the life and teachings of President Perón
and explain their significance for the country. This
resulted in an attempt to lift *Peronismo* from the
status of a political doctrine to an article of faith
for all Argentines. The implication of this was
that what Perón and his government did was not
to be questioned, not even by the church.

During this episode the influence (both good and bad) of Eva Perón, previous to her death, was recognized by writers of Argentine history. There was little doubt of her popularity and influence in working-class quarters. Also, she won for herself a unique place in matters of state as well as in foreign affairs. Yet, immediately following her death the power and influence of President Perón appears to have continued without abatement.

The cleavage in this alliance took even more serious turns following the election of Perón for his second term of office in 1952. The Catholic Church had shown suspicion and distrust of Perón's widespread organization of the nation's youth. An Associated Press dispatch from Buenos Aires on November 28, 1954, reported growing tension between the government and the church. Perón had accused three Catholic bishops and twenty-one priests as "open enemies" trying to infiltrate labor and student organizations in a way to harm his regime. In December the police refused permission for the scheduled annual procession through downtown Buenos Aires of clergy and laymen honoring the Virgin Mary. During the same month a law was passed by the Argentine Congress and signed by the President legalizing divorce in Argentina, which up to this date had never been legally granted in the Republic.

The gap between the Argentine government and the Roman Catholic Church continued to widen during 1955. Early in the year the National Congress approved a bill providing for the election of a constitutional convention to make a partial reform of the constitution, eliminating all references to relations between church and state. The intent of this bill was to end the status of the Roman Catholic Church as a state church, which since the founding of the republic had received support from the government.

This provision looking toward the separation of church and state was designed to end the financial support of the federal government to the Catholic Church and to cancel the stipulation that the President and Vice-President of the republic be Roman Catholics. During the early months of 1955 the Argentine government also terminated the church's privilege to use the Argentine radio for Catholic programs and abolished the Bureau of Religious Education in the Ministry of Education. Subsequently the Congress voted to abolish religious instruction in the public schools.

By the middle of 1955 it became evident that opposition within the country to the Perón government was much more complex and went much deeper than the cleavage with the Roman Catholic Church. In June the storm of revolution broke when uprisings took place in several parts of the republic, led by the navy and the air force. Later, other parts of the army joined in the revolt. The Perón government fell on September 19 and the new government headed by Major General Eduardo Lonardi was inaugurated on September 23. A few weeks later, November 13, General Lonardi was overthrown by a palace revolution and Major General Pedro Eugenio Aramburu was sworn in as Provisional President of the Argentine Republic.

CHAPTER III

Protestant Beginnings
in Argentina

Protestantism as a cultural force in South America was first felt during and following the revolutionary period when immigration and colonization from Europe took place. An effort on the part of the French Huguenots to organize a colony on the continent early in the sixteenth century did not prove a success, and nearly two centuries passed before Protestant Christianity again became represented in South America.

It was during the first quarter of the nineteenth century that Protestantism began actively to extend its influence into Argentina. To the British and Foreign Bible Society belongs the honor of having introduced Argentina to the perennial source of Christian thought and experience. "Not with the sword, but with a Book, did the new Christians appear."[1] The forerunner of Evangelical Christianity in Argentina was James Thomson, a Scotsman who arrived in Buenos Aires in 1818,[2] which was shortly after the Argentine revolution.[3] He taught school and sold Bibles. Thomson left no trained successors and no permanent work and yet he symbolized two of the most important contribu-

[1]John A. Mackay, op. cit., p. 232.
[2]Thomson was sent out by the British and Foreign Bible Society.
[3]The revolution in which Argentina broke away from Spain took place in 1810, although the constitution was not written until six or seven years later.

tions of the Evangelical movement to the people
of the area, namely, popular education and the
Bible. In Protestant countries, the two go hand in
hand and are the pillars of democracy.

In these early years, however, Evangelical Christianity was introduced into the religious life and
tradition of Argentina largely by foreign colonists
from Protestant countries who established themselves on the Atlantic seaboard. The first of these
bodies to obtain a foothold was the Anglican Church,
which held its first service in the English language
in Buenos Aires in 1824. Other bodies which established themselves along with their colonists were the
Scots Presbyterians in 1829, the German Evangelical
Church in 1834, the Waldensians in 1857, and the
Welsh Church in the Territory of Chubut in 1866.
A number of other colonial churches have been
established more recently.

The work of mission boards from the United
States began in the same period in which Evangelical churches from other countries were established
in Argentina. The breaking away from Spain and
the setting up of republican forms of government
by the peoples of South America opened the way
for Protestant missions. The close similarity between the constitution of the United States and
that of Argentina was a binding symbol and
awakened deep interest and sympathy among the
peoples of the two republics. The conviction grew
that the time was ripe for mission boards to extend
their work to the republics to the south, and small
beginnings were made in Argentina in the first half
of the nineteenth century. The Board of Foreign
Missions of the Presbyterian Church in the United

States of America was the first to attempt to establish its work in Argentina. In April, 1826, the first missionary of the Presbyterian Church reached Buenos Aires. This first attempt to establish a mission did not succeed and another effort was made in 1854. Neither of these attempts of the Presbyterian Church of the U.S.A. was successful and they abandoned the enterprise in 1859, leaving the field to the Scots Presbyterian Church. The Methodist Church from the United States established work in Buenos Aires in 1836 and with the exception of the two years between 1841 and 1843 the work has been continuous.

Following these beginnings, other Evangelical bodies established work in Argentina in the latter half of the nineteenth and early part of the twentieth century. Among the bodies establishing work there were the Seventh-Day Adventists in 1897, the Christian and Missionary Alliance in 1900, the Evangelical Union in 1898, the Southern Baptists in 1903, the Disciples of Christ in 1906, the United Lutheran Church in 1918, and the Mennonites in 1919. Other religious groups have since opened work in the Argentine Republic.

While many changes in the government of Argentina following the revolution and the establishment of the Republic made it possible for Evangelical Christianity to establish itself in the country, the privilege of religious freedom and the opportunity for these churches to do work freely were won slowly. The law prohibiting the teaching of religion in the language of the country by the Protestant churches remained on the statute books for

a number of years. It was not until 1867 that this
law was changed, permitting Protestant bodies to
carry on their worship and services in the Spanish
language.

John G. Thomson, remembered as the pioneer
Protestant preacher in the Spanish language, was
born in Scotland June 3, 1843, and when eight years
old went with his parents to Buenos Aires to reside.
His mother was Presbyterian and his father Methodist. John became converted when very young. Feeling the call of the ministry, he went to the United
States, where he studied at Ohio Wesleyan. It was
from that institution he received the degree of
doctor of divinity. After six years' absence, he returned to Buenos Aires in 1866.

The first Spanish-speaking preaching service of
the Evangelicals was held early in 1867 in the Boca,
on Almirante Brown Street, in Buenos Aires. The
service was held in a school conducted by Doña
Fermina Leon de Aldeder. An Evangelical Sunday
school, organized the same year, and carried on in
the Spanish language, was the first not only in
Buenos Aires but in all South America to be conducted in that language. The work was hindered,
however, by an epidemic of cholera and, as Dr.
Thomson said, a worse plague of *sacerdotalismo y
fannatismo*. The first Spanish-speaking Evangelical service held in a church building was on May
25, 1867, when services were conducted by Dr. Thomson in the church on Cangallo Street. This event
has been remembered as an historical occasion by
the Protestants of the Republic. This, of course,
gave great impetus to the missionary churches in
their work of preaching and teaching.

This movement of the Protestant churches and of
mission boards from other countries was extended
throughout South America. By the end of the
nineteenth century, Protestantism had its representatives in all Latin American countries. However,
the friends of Latin America, in their desire that
the country should have an opportunity to become
acquainted with the full gospel of Christ, had to
convince the Protestant world that Latin America
was a mission field. The first World Congress of
Protestant Missions, which met in Edinburgh, Scotland, in 1910, made no place on the program for
consideration of the religious situation in Latin
America. So a special Congress, bringing together
representatives of the missionary societies working
in Latin America, was convened in Panama in 1916.
From that Congress dates a new era in the history
of Evangelical activity in the southern continent.
The field was surveyed, existing work was co-
ordinated, special territorial and other responsibilities were accepted by different missionary organizations. Subsequent Congresses held in Montevideo
in 1925, in Havana in 1929, and in Buenos Aires
in 1949 carried forward what was begun in Panama.[4]

The work of cooperation which received formal
recognition at the Panama Congress in 1916, has
continued to exist and go forward in Latin America.
The Committee on Cooperation in Latin America[5]
has effectively carried on this cooperative effort
among the Evangelical churches. Its head offices

[4]Mae Yoho Ward, *Disciples of Christ in Latin America and Jamaica* (Indianapolis: The United Christian Missionary Society,
1951), p. 5.

[5]The Committee on Cooperation, organized previous to the Congress
on Christian Work, held in Panama in 1916, represented most of the
Protestant Churches doing mission work in Latin America. See
Chapter V.

have been maintained in New York City with regional offices in many of the Latin American countries. The regional organization for the River Plate Republics was established, soon after the Panama Congress, with headquarters in Montevideo, Uruguay. In 1926 the regional headquarters were transferred from Montevideo to Buenos Aires where the work of the local committee continued until the organization of the Confederation of Evangelical Churches in 1939. This new body then took over the work previously conducted by the Committee on Cooperation in this region and has subsequently served as its agent in the River Plate Republics.

The Confederation of Evangelical Churches is an indigenous organization which came into being at the initiation of the churches in the River Plate Republics. It elects its governing board and chooses its executive officers. It enlarged the scope of cooperative work by bringing into the new body a larger group of communions and by extending the radius of activity. This has made more effective the cooperative work within Argentina and, through representatives sent to world gatherings in other lands, has brought the Protestant bodies in the River Plate Republics more fully into the ecumenical movement.

PART TWO: THE DISCIPLE STORY

CHAPTER IV

The Disciples Open Work in an Expanding City
1906-1916

It is not easy for a new Christian mission to get a foothold in a great city in any country. This was uniquely true in the growing metropolis of Buenos Aires at the beginning of the twentieth century where scores of churches were in evidence and where religious holidays were commonplace events. There the name of Christ was perhaps known to everybody and most of the people had been baptized into the Roman Catholic church.

When new Protestant missionaries arrived, the people of the country must have asked themselves, "Why do Protestant missionaries come to our city? What additional light or what new religious interpretation do they think they can give us? What can they tell us about the life and message of Jesus Christ that we do not already know?" These and many other questions no doubt occurred to them. But the conditions were not as simple as these questions might imply. Gradually over many years, for reasons explained in Chapter II, many of the people in Argentina had lost faith in the Roman Catholic Church. Those who continued loyal to the church often gave their allegiance without much questioning and duly went to Confession and Mass once a year so that the services of the church would be theirs when final sickness and death came to them. But the general tone of the country was becoming more materialistic and people were raising questions about the meaning of their Christian faith.

One might better visualize what it means to work in such a situation by imagining himself starting a mission work under similar conditions in his own country. Such a comparison will help one to understand something of the difficulty of opening mission work in any country with an established religion. Imagine a couple of Argentines arriving in Chicago, renting a residence on a side street and putting up a bulletin board in front stating that church services would be held at certain hours. How many and what kind of people would attend the services? To make any progress in the community and to establish contacts with individuals the missionaries had to get children together in kindergartens, day schools, and through them get into homes; or they had to learn of a family here and there that had already been touched by some Protestant worker and was more or less sympathetic to Protestant ideas.

The first missionaries in a country realize that these conditions are to be faced and that indifference and opposition must be overcome. So as the first Disciple missionaries began their task in Argentina they worked patiently and persistently and the Church slowly took hold. The results of these early endeavors bore fruit, and, as will be evident later, there has developed a fine corps of indigenous leaders.

The challenge of Argentina was part of a larger appeal of all Latin America. Work by the Disciples of Christ had previously been established in Mexico

in 1895 and in Puerto Rico in 1899. The summons
to missionary service in these countries had not
only aroused Disciple leaders in the United States,
but had stirred young Christians who were willing
to offer their lives for the cause of Christ in these
lands. Mr. and Mrs. Willis J. Burner were the first
missionaries of the Disciples of Christ to accept the
call to Argentina. They sailed from New York City
on September 13, 1905, and reached Buenos Aires on
October 23. Both Willis J. Burner and Lulu Burr
Burner were natives of Illinois. Mr. Burner went
to Argentina as a living link of the Union Avenue
Christian Church, St. Louis, Missouri, while Mrs.
Burner was the representative of the University
Place Christian Church of Champaign, Illinois.

The missionary work of the Disciples of Christ
was begun in Argentina under auspices of the Christian Woman's Board of Missions. After the organization of The United Christian Missionary Society
in 1920, the oversight of this work was carried on
under the Department of Latin America in the
Division of Foreign Missions of the newly formed
Society.

Previous to the going of Mr. and Mrs. Burner to
Argentina, Miss Hallie Embree, a Disciple, had gone
to this field as an interdenominational missionary
under the Christian and Missionary Alliance. She
was a native of Kentucky and a member of the
Christian church at Berea from which she received
some financial aid for mission work in Argentina.
In 1904 she wrote from Argentina to the Christian
Woman's Board of Missions expressing her willing-
ness to serve as a missionary under that Board. She
was apparently located in or near the city of Buenos

Aires. Miss Embree continued to lay the needs of Argentina before the Christian Woman's Board of Missions and was probably influential in bringing about its decision to open work in South America. She apparently was associated with the Disciple Mission for a brief period but soon returned to work under the Christian and Missionary Alliance. At its annual meeting in 1904, the Christian Woman's Board of Missions approved a motion to open mission work in the Argentine Republic.

When Mr. and Mrs. Burner, with their three children, arrived in Argentina in the autumn of 1905, they selected as their place of residence the city of La Plata, the capital of the Province of Buenos Aires. La Plata lies some thirty-five miles southeast of the Federal Capital, Buenos Aires. For some months they lived there, spending their time profitably in language study and in exploring a location for permanent establishment of the Mission. Study revealed that three missions were already working in La Plata while many other localities were unoccupied. So they located in Belgrano, a rapidly growing suburb of Buenos Aires. Belgrano was soon to be incorporated as a part of the Federal Capital of the Republic of Argentina.

The Methodists had started work in Belgrano at an earlier time but this had been abandoned before the Burners decided to go there. In writing later about this move, Mr. Burner explained and justified the choice of location when he wrote:

. . . I am sure our active missionary work should begin in Buenos Aires. . . . This great city is the center of things in this part of the world. For our first mission we have selected a part of the city where there are four thousand people without a mission. At first we will preach to a procession, as people will not attend with any regularity. Our Sunday School will be subject to the same affliction. It is very probable that after the first curiosity is satisfied, the attendance will diminish for a season. But sooner or later someone will become interested and will defy public opinion by becoming a Protestant. It will be a slow process to collect the first nucleus of believers. But in time the teaching and the preaching do their work and the circle of interest widens.[1]

Later experience verified the correctness of this evaluation by Mr. Burner.

Upon locating in Belgrano in 1906 Mr. and Mrs. Burner first opened work in a rented dwelling on the corner of Olazábal and O'Higgins Streets where the work continued for two years. This location was described by Señora (Mrs.) Elena Colmegna de Azzati in the following way:

> It was an old house at the time, with a large living room with high-barred windows, which was used as a hall for preaching services. The large vestibule and wide carved door gave it a dignified appearance but, since the street was dark and there was little traffic, the place was gloomy. This was perhaps the reason why, in spite of the fact that the door was always open, only a few at first attended the services. But the interest and consecration of those few were outstanding, for in many cases they walked as many as thirty blocks, not on paved streets either, such as we have today, in order to attend the services.[2]

This was an humble beginning of what developed into a significant work. The first sermon in this newly opened chapel was preached on Sunday, December 9, 1906, by an Englishman, Mr. Airth, who had affiliated himself with the new group of Evangelical Christians. The first baptism to take place in this emerging church was that of John G. Penman, a Scottish engineer, who was baptized on July 27, 1907. This baptism was performed by Edwin Wyle in a Swiss Baptist Church.

[1]Quoted in *They Went to Latin America* (Indianapolis: The United Christian Missionary Society, 1947), p. 61.

[2]From an unpublished article written in 1954. Translated by Samuel S. McWilliams.

Edwin Wyle, born near London, England, the son of a Baptist clergyman, was inspired with missionary zeal at an early age. He was educated in London where he entered into his journalistic profession. After traveling around the world, he was appointed first to Africa, and afterward to South America, where he served as a journalist. In 1907, Mr. Burner wrote from Buenos Aires that one of the church members, Edwin Wyle, had recently come from England to take a place on the *Victoria Evangelical Press,* and that he wished Mr. Wyle might be connected with our mission as he was a faithful preacher of the Christian Church. This wish was granted and in December of that year Mr. and Mrs. Wyle became our second missionary couple in Argentina. As a part of his work Mr. Wyle taught English in our school. Because of failing health the Wyles were compelled to leave Argentina in 1909 and return to England. While their ministry in that field was brief, it was fruitful and they contributed much to the growth of the work during the year they served there, and their going was felt deeply by the other missionaries.[3]

On August 16, 1907, Manuel Andrade and his wife together with Francisco Racio were the first Argentines to be baptized in the rented building of the new Mission. Mr. Burner's ingenuity in improvizing a metal baptistry had made this possible. Señor (Mr.) Andrade and his wife were the first Argentine Disciples to open their home for cottage prayer meetings. The constant and enthusiastic

[3]Mr. and Mrs. Wyle later came to the United States, where he was pastor of Disciple churches until his death in 1952. Their son, Ewart, is a minister and has served First Christian Church, Tyler, Texas, and, more recently, Country Club Christian Church, Kansas City, Missouri.

work of Sra. Andrade as a lay Christian won for her special recognition in the neighborhood as an Evangelical. Of equal importance to the baptismal service was the first communion service conducted in Spanish by the Disciples of Christ in Argentina. This took place on August 25, 1907.[4]

From the corner of Olazábal and O'Higgins Streets, the Mission was moved to 2347 Cabildo Street. Cabildo was then, and still is, the principal street in Belgrano. The dwelling rented there was larger, more inviting and comfortable than the previous building. So the work grew more rapidly and the congregation began to appear more like a church. The attendance was increased not only from newly converted families, but also from the attendance of Evangelical Christians who were living in the community. An important event in the life of Mr. and Mrs. Burner during these years was the birth of their fourth child, Lulu Elena.

The results of these beginning years are not fully told by the success or failure of renting or buying buildings, nor by the struggle against indifference or open opposition. Rather, the lasting results are recorded by the lives of those who accepted Christ and were saved through his redeeming love. Some of the experiences of those years are told by Sra. Elena Colmegna de Azzati, wife of a Disciple minister and the mother of four children. She has been a loyal and active supporter of the Disciple work from its early beginnings. Writing in 1947 she said:

For me it is interesting to go back in memory to the days of my childhood, see the friends of long ago and relive the experiences

[4]Willis J. Burner, *South America, Our Mission in Argentina* (Indianapolis: Christian Woman's Board of Missions, 1912), p. 35.

of those days, for I was only a child when I began attending the
Sunday school back in 1907. Sometimes there were only three
or four of us. At that time the church occupied a large old
house on the corner of Olazábal and O'Higgins. The door was
always open as an invitation to the passersby to enter, but at first
only a few accepted that invitation. Our dear pastor, Mr. Burner,
in spite of difficulties with the Spanish language, was a tireless
worker. That first year there were seven baptisms and we had our
first public communion service in Spanish.[5]

Personnel is essential if new mission work is to
grow and develop. This need of workers highlighted
the importance of the arrival in Buenos Aires on
February 11, 1910, of two new missionaries, Mrs.
Maria Reynolds Ford and Miss Zona Smith.

With the coming of these missionaries an added
impetus was given to the work which resulted in
the enlargement of the Mission. In the spring of
1910 a house was rented in the section of the city
adjacent to Belgrano known as Colegiales. The
first preaching service at this location was held on
March 12, 1910. This laid the foundation for a
second congregation, now the Colegiales Church, in
Buenos Aires. In this new location the work started
with preaching services on Saturday nights and the
Bible school on Sunday mornings. Later two
preaching services and church school were held
weekly. In addition to services in Spanish, for a
time services were held in English.

Mrs. Maria Reynolds Ford was assigned a major
responsibility in the supervision and guidance of
this new work in Colegiales. Mrs. Ford was from
Morrison, Tennessee. She had lived in Mexico and
served with the Disciple Mission in Puerto Rico for
five years before going to Argentina. Her knowledge of the Spanish language, acquired in her pre-

[5]Elena Colmegna de Azzati, *River Plate Reflections* [June], 1947,
p. (3).

vious work, enabled her to enter into the work immediately upon reaching Argentina. She took over the supervision of the Sunday school, visited in homes in the community, and taught a Bible class for women and girls in addition to other duties. However, the climate did not agree with Mrs. Ford and after a short stay it was decided that she should resign her work in Buenos Aires and return home.

Miss Zona Smith was born in Knoxville, Iowa, and received an academic degree from Drake University in 1904. Twenty years later she was elected to Phi Beta Kappa. Her service to the Evangelical churches in Argentina was longer than that of any other missionary of the Disciples. She is the only Disciple missionary who is buried in the Argentine. Miss Smith came to her work in Argentina without a knowledge of the language and so her first duty was the study of Spanish, in which she progressed rapidly and was soon able to enter actively into the work. She shared in the evangelistic and educational work both in Belgrano and in Colegiales. As part of her work, she taught in the Sunday school and organized and taught special courses. One year she made over 400 helpful visits in Argentine homes! Perhaps the outstanding achievement of Miss Smith during her first term of service was the translation and publication in Spanish of the book, *God and Me,* by Dr. Peter Ainslie, the Spanish title being *Dios y Yo.* She was helped with the translation by Román García, a member of the Belgrano congregation and a lay preacher. She published the book in Buenos Aires at her own expense in 1914. This was the first important literary work in Spanish attempted by the Disciples in Argentina.

While the foundation was being laid for a congregation of the Disciples in these early years, the welcome word was received from the Mission Board in the United States to purchase a lot for a permanent location. This lot was bought for $4,400 and became the site of the present building in Belgrano on Cramer Street. The problem was then faced of erecting an adequate building for $10,000. This was done with remarkable success and the building which was completed in 1911 housed the chapel with a seating capacity of 140 and rooms for a day school. On the second floor was a five-room residence, bathroom, and kitchen. Writing about this building at the time of dedication, Miss Zona Smith said: "This is the only property of the Disciples of Christ in all this great continent of South America, and ours is the second Evangelical American Board to own property in Argentina, the Methodist Board being the first."[6] The original plans provided for an enlargement of this building on a section of the lot left vacant, but this plan has never been realized.

The dedicatory service for this new building was held on January 22, 1911. The occasion was one of great joy as the new Mission set apart this building for worship and Christian teaching and offered it to the community as the permanent location for their services and educational activities. For this service of dedication the chapel was filled to capacity, which indicated that the Mission was well received in the community. Willis J. Burner, the pastor, preached the dedicatory sermon. The benches of the chapel, the pulpit and other furniture

[6]From an unpublished article written in 1911.

were contributed by the members of this small congregation. As congregations of Disciples developed in other sections of the city during these early decades, the Belgrano congregation became the mother church and was looked to for leadership and counsel.

The dedication was followed by eight days of evangelistic services. Among ministers invited to preach during the services was Señor Francisco Penzotti, the secretary of the American Bible Society for South America. Much interest was manifested in the meetings and there was good attendance thoughout the week. There were several confessions of faith and during the first month in the new chapel a total of twenty-six new members were received into the membership of the congregation by baptism. Witnessing for Evangelical Christianity was not easy for many of these new converts. One who was a member of the congregation at the time of the dedication recalls in the following statement the faith and conviction of these Christians:

I do not remember well enough to recount at this time many of the happenings in the neighborhood, but I can tell of the enthusiasm with which the first converts embraced their new religion. Many of them had to give up the Roman Catholic faith but they did so with determination and courage. I remember the case of a janitor in an elementary school not far from the church who, after relinquishing his former faith, was visited by the Catholic priest, and it is humorous to recount that our brother, when he had a service in his own home, invited that priest to attend, which, of course, he did not do.[7]

Soon after the new building was dedicated, a day school was opened in the rooms planned for that purpose. This school started on February 1, 1911,

[7]Elena Colmegna de Azzati, from an unpublished article written in 1954. Translated by Samuel S. McWilliams.

with fifteen students enrolled. Miss Zona Smith
was in charge of the school and was assisted by an
Argentine teacher, Señorita (Miss) Margarita
Mainar.[8]

Another phase of Christian work which was initiated soon after the congregation occupied the
church building on Cramer Street was the organization of a Christian Endeavor Society under the
leadership of Miss Zona Smith. This was the first
Christian Endeavor Society conducted in the Spanish language in Argentina. It made a deep impression upon the lives of young people who became
members and in later years they recalled with enthusiasm these earlier experiences.

This beginning, however, could not be measured
by the number of services held or the frequency and
attendance of classes. Much pastoral work was
done and personal friendships were cultivated. This
all required office work, publicity materials, study
courses in Spanish, and literature for distribution.
A paper published monthly, entitled *La Luz y la
Verdad (The Light and the Truth)*, carried articles
on religious subjects, contained notices of meetings,
and other items of information. Its distribution
was largely to the homes of members and to friends
through personal contact.

After seven years of faithful pioneer service, the
Burners returned to the United States in 1912 for
an overdue furlough. During the early years of this
term of service the responsibility of initiating and
conducting the work of the Disciple Mission rested
almost entirely with Mr. and Mrs. Burner. They
carried this responsibility to their credit and with

[8]Willis J. Burner, *op. cit.*, p. 45.

praise from those who remember them forty years later. Along with the tasks that seemed difficult and monotonous, there were also happenings that were unusual and humorous. Stories are told of how the mischievous boys of the community would delight in disturbing the services in the Belgrano church, especially during the summer months when the doors and windows were open because of the heat. Sometimes these boys would enter the chapel while services were going on. The following incident happened one Sunday evening:

> We were surprised to have Mr. Burner stop preaching, jump over the railing of the platform, and disappear through the doorway. Many thought he had gone crazy but before we had recovered from our surprise we saw him reappear almost exhausted, with his arms full of Bibles and hymnals. What had happened? The mischief makers had taken the books from the shelves in the entryway during the service, and Mr. Burner, after a short run, had succeeded in recovering them from the ''thieves.''[9]

The education of their children, and Mrs. Burner's health, made it inadvisable for them to return to Argentina and their resignation followed. They settled in Columbia, Missouri, where for some years Mr. Burner was professor of sociology at the University of Missouri.

This solid beginning of the work of the Disciples in Argentina which assured development in future years was due to the careful planning and the devoted service of Mr. and Mrs. Burner. The tribute to them by one of the Argentine Disciple pastors, Sr. Feliciano A. Sarli, is worthy of mention. ''Mr. and Mrs. Burner had an intensive evangelistic spirit which, along with devoted personal work, in spite of language handicaps, brought prompt results. . . .

---

[9]Colmegna de Azzati, unpublished *op. cit.*

The ardent work of Mr. Burner and his able colleagues, Mrs. Ford and Miss Smith, with God's blessing, were the channels through which the work made progress in Belgrano and the new work was progressively established in Colegiales.'"[10]

Previous to the sailing of the Burners, Mr. and Mrs. Tolbert F. Reavis had arrived in Buenos Aires to take over the superintendency of the work. Tolbert F. Reavis was born in Lewisburg, Tennessee, and later moved with his parents to Canton, Missouri. Mabel Yokley Reavis was born in Buffalo, Missouri. Their study of the Spanish language before going to the field made it possible for them to enter soon into the work. After a residence of three months in the new field, Mr. Reavis assumed the superintendency of the evangelistic work. They gave thirteen years of devoted service to the mission work in Argentina.

The first decade of the work in Argentina was difficult and required patience, loyalty, and a profound Christian faith. The results could not be measured by the numbers of persons won, nor merely by the program which was initiated. Rather it was through consecrated effort that a secure foundation for the work was laid. A permanent location had been established, a day school formed, a wide circle of friends enlisted, and a growing congregation of Christian believers organized.

[10]*El Mensajero, 30 Años de Trabajo en el Plata,* April, 1937, p. 7. Translated by J. D. Montgomery.

CHAPTER V

Enlarged Visions and New Adventures

1916-1926

Enlarged vision lifted the horizons to new fields of endeavor and a passion for greater service led to new adventures. These are the elements which characterized the work of the Disciples of Christ in Argentina during the years from 1916 to 1926. C. Manly Morton, writing from Argentina at the beginning of this decade, expressed the enthusiasm that was moving Disciple missionaries with these words, "The future of our work in South America looks brighter and more inviting and compelling than it has ever seemed to us since we began to study this field. A broad but definite program has been mapped out. The Mission has been organized. . . ."[1] This vision motivated the Disciple missionaries in Argentina and was part of a wider outreach of all Protestant forces working in Latin America.

The Congress on Christian Work, held in Panama, February, 1916, formulated a new strategy of Protestant mission work in Latin America which gave impetus to the enlarged task of Christian missions in those lands. This Congress exemplified a spirit of fairness and of diligent endeavor as its members together faced difficult and perplexing problems. If the Protestant churches were to meet the challenge

---

[1] *Missionary Tidings*, Oct., 1917, p. 211.

in Latin America, this congenial and earnest spirit must permeate the various missions and church relationships. The conviction of those attending the Congress was that it "has breathed new courage and hope into the hearts of lonely and scattered workers. It has led to a cleared discernment of the need of cooperation in tasks which are too great to be compassed in aloofness. It has sounded a call to a fuller fellowship of faith and race and to a recognition of the fact that not geography, nor political sympathy, nor commercial interests, nor science, nor trade, but only Christ can ever unite the nationals of the North and South or of the East and West."[2] The Disciples of Christ entered fully into the development and execution of this new strategy of mission work. Their future work in the Republics of the River Plate (Argentina, Paraguay, and Uruguay) for decades to come was to be guided by this policy which was formulated as a result of the Panama Congress on Christian Work.

The awakened interest in Christian work in Latin America which had led to the organization of the Congress in Panama had at the same time stimulated the Christian Woman's Board of Missions to enlarge and strengthen its work in Argentina. Funds were needed and secured, but perhaps a greater response was that of volunteers who enlisted. Unusually talented young men and women completed their training and were ready for missionary service in Argentina. As a result of the challenge of this new field and the awakened interest, the largest number of missionaries ever to serve during one decade in Argentina were on the field.

---

[2]Panama Congress 1916, *Christian Work in Latin America* (3 vols.; New York: The Missionary Education Movement, 1917), I, 33. Used by permission of Friendship Press, Inc.

In this decade, the first visit of a Christian Woman's Board of Missions executive was made when Mrs. Anna R. Atwater, in company with her sister, Miss Harriett Robinson, visited Argentina in 1921. This was an important visit which gave Mrs. Atwater an opportunity to become acquainted with the Disciple Mission in Argentina and to offer counsel for the future development of the work in this growing station. Dr. S. Guy Inman, executive secretary of the Committee on Cooperation in Latin America, was also in Buenos Aires and shared in the deliberations regarding plans for the future work of the Disciples of Christ. Following their visit in Argentina, Mrs. Atwater and Miss Robinson with Dr. Inman, who had been requested to accompany them, visited Paraguay, where important issues were to be faced and far-reaching decisions made.

On October 5, 1916, Clement Manly and Selah Louise Beam Morton arrived in Buenos Aires as missionaries. He came originally from North Carolina and she from Kansas. A year later, November 13, 1917, Robert Bruce and Mary Hilton Lemmon reached Buenos Aires, both being natives of Nebraska. In 1918 Miss Mary Irene Orvis joined the missionary group in Argentina, being also a native of North Carolina and having served one term with the Disciple Mission in Mexico. The following year, November, 1919, Samuel S. and Alice Terrissa Sheplee McWilliams arrived in Buenos Aires, both from Iowa. In the spring of 1920, Charles A. and Mary Adelaide Vannoy reached Argentina, their respective native states being Indiana and Iowa.

Fred W. and Mary Ingle Hughes arrived in
Buenos Aires from the United States in December,
1920. Mr. Hughes was born in Farnworth, England,
and Mrs. Hughes in Iowa. They spent one year
in Buenos Aires, studying the language and teaching in *Colegio* Ward before joining the staff of
Colegio Internacional in Asunción, Paraguay.[3]

Miss Ruth Ella Fish, who hailed from California,
arrived in Buenos Aires in the autumn of 1922. The
same year, in November, Abner and Olive Adamson
Johnson reached Argentina, he from Missouri and
she from Iowa. Howard T. and Leona McMahan
Holroyd joined the missionary force in Buenos
Aires in 1923, both natives of Ohio.

With the enlarged visions and the awakened interests, the work of the Disciples which had started
a decade earlier began to extend its radius of activities. As the Mission entered this second decade,
it owned but one piece of property, the Belgrano
Church building on Cramer Street. In 1918 two
lots were bought on the corner of Federico Lacroze
and Zapiola which later became the site of the Colegiales Church. On April 7, 1918, Mr. and Mrs.
Tolbert F. Reavis, with the aid of Sra. Emilia
Echauriz and her two sons, opened a new work in
the section of Buenos Aires known as La Paternal.
In this effort, Mr. Reavis was assisted by three
Union Seminary students. This section of the city
lies about halfway between the Belgrano church and
the Seminary. In describing the opening of this
work, Mr. Reavis wrote, "It was a beautiful early
autumnal day [the seasons in Argentina are in

---

[3]Mr. and Mrs. Hughes returned to the United States on furlough
in 1954, following which Mr. Hughes, having reached the age of retirement, did ad-interim pastoral work.

reverse to the United States]. The very sun and air seemed to bless the occasion. Thirty-two children came in and stayed through the Sunday school service, and almost as many looked on from the outside. At night every seat was taken and between thirty and forty people stood up. The door and street were also full. Most of them had never heard a gospel sermon."[4] Mr. and Mrs. Reavis were able to open this work since they could turn over the labor in Colegiales to Mr. and Mrs. Robert B. Lemmon and Miss Zona Smith. This ministry in La Paternal was the beginning of what later developed into the congregation now known as the Villa Mitre Christian Church.

On the same Sunday, April 7, 1918, that the work was started in La Paternal, C. Manly Morton opened another new ministry in the section of the city known as Villa Devoto. Shortly after the program was begun, Mr. Morton wrote:

... This work is located in an exceedingly strong Roman Catholic community. The second Lord's day after we opened a priest came and stood in the street just below our hall and as the children came out of Bible School gave them beautifully lithographed pictures of the Virgin and told them that that was a bad place for them to go and that they must not have anything to do with those evangelicals, for they were bad people and would lead them to the devil. He told them that he was giving them cards that day, but that if they ever returned to that Bible School he would never give them another card. When we saw what he was doing someone remarked: "There was a saloon in this same building for four years. I wonder if that or any other priest ever came here to distribute literature and to tell the fathers of these children that the saloon was a bad place and that they should not go to such a place, or that it would lead them to the devil?" We were anxious to know the effect upon the attendance for the next Lord's day. But the next week we had one more than on that Lord's day, the next ten more, and the next thirty-three more, so that although

---

[4]*Missionary Tidings,* June, 1918, p. 53.

some were kept away others came to take their places, and we feel that we have won in the first skirmish. We pray that we may be as successful in the big battle which we know is before us![5]

Mr. Morton assumed this work of the Sunday school and services in Villa Devoto along with his ministry with the Belgrano church by leaving the Belgrano Sunday school in charge of Mrs. Morton and Argentine assistants. The Villa Devoto preaching services were held on Saturday evenings so that he could be at Belgrano Sunday evenings. The work at Villa Devoto continued for several years but was later closed for lack of sufficient budget.

A congregation of Italian brethren which along with its pastor, Blas A. Maradei, had been affiliated with the Southern Baptists united with the Disciple Mission early in 1915 where it found a more congenial fellowship. In the fall of 1916 Mr. Reavis wrote that he had recently helped this congregation to move from its location on Araoz Street to Rivera Street where there was a more adequate building with ample room. He said of this group of Christians, "We call this the 'Italian band,' not because the work is in Italian, for in fact the services are nearly all conducted in Spanish, but because the majority of the members are of that nationality. They are noble Christians and are doing a great work. It is about as nearly Christian in tone and character as any work we have ever known."[6] He spoke well of the pastor and his leadership.

In Saavedra, a section of the city adjacent to Belgrano, evangelistic work was opened in 1919 by Antonio De Césare who was a student in the

[5]*Ibid*, Aug., 1918, p. 127.
[6]*Ibid*, Nov., 1916, p. 276.

Seminary. The work began as a small Sunday
school in the home of Sr. José Urso, a faithful
member of the Belgrano congregation. One who
knew Sr. José Urso personally wrote the following
about his conversion and his subsequent loyalty to
and support of the church.

One of the most interesting characters in our Cramer Street
Church, Buenos Aires, Argentina, is an Italian peón named José
Urso, more familiarly and universally called Don José.

He lives some twenty-two blocks from the church, but seldom
misses Sunday school, communion or preaching service. He does
not have money to ride on the streetcar so he often walks that
distance back and forth three times on Sunday and he very seldom
comes without bringing some friend or neighbor with him. Perhaps
no other lay member of the church has brought as many people
to the church as has Don José.

When our work was first established in Buenos Aires, Don José
was one of the toughest characters in that section of the city. He
was seldom sober and scarcely ever went home without beating his
wife. It is generally supposed that his cruel treatment was the
indirect cause of his first wife's death.

Saturday nights and Sundays were his especially high days and
often every penny of his week's earnings went for drink or at the
gaming table.

One cold winter's Sunday night, after a night and day of especial
debauchery and while yet in a drunken stupor, a friend invited him
to attend the church service at our Cramer Street mission. In a
half dare-devil spirit and thinking of it as a place where he could
sit down, he entered. He slept through most of the service, but
somehow the songs and the words of welcome made an impression
on him. The next Sunday night he came back and this time not so
drunk. Many weeks he continued to come. The strange message
seemed to fascinate and charm him. He could not understand it all,
but he understood enough to know that his life was all wrong and
that he must clean it up. One night he arose from his place and
came forward and said, "Lord, if you take me and make a man
of what is left, I will serve you." From that day to this no
one has had any doubts as to the genuineness of the conversion of
Don José. The large family of children are being raised up in the
church and it is seldom too hot or too cold for his pew to remain
unoccupied or for the long line of little Ursos to be absent from
their places in Bible school or church.

After his conversion Don José was much troubled that he could not read. He wanted to know more about the Bible. He was too old and too ignorant, he thought, to learn through the ordinary channels, so he began to pray that the Lord might open his understanding so that he might read and understand the Bible. And the Lord who had saved him from sin taught him to read. I do not know how much effort he himself put forth and I am very sure that his efforts at reading are many times most humorous; still, as far as he is concerned, his ability to read is a miracle and a direct answer to his prayer. And I believe he is right.

Indeed, the gospel is the power of God unto salvation.[7]

Later as the attendance at this Saavedra Sunday school grew, a room was rented near the home of Sr. Urso at 3107 Arias Street where the work continued. When Sr. De Césare was transferred to Asunción, Paraguay, to work with *Colegio Internacional,* Feliciano A. Sarli was given charge of this work which grew and was the beginning of the Saavedra Christian Church which now has an attractive church building in the neighborhood where it first started.

This outreach revealed the evangelistic passion of those who were leading the Argentine Mission. The reports of the Mission for 1923 stated that there were eight preaching points, although the Belgrano church was the only building owned by the Mission. But the lack of buildings did not deter an aggressive, creative outlook toward the future and the upbuilding of Christ's Kingdom. The work in the Belgrano church under the leadership of C. Manly and Selah Morton was making progress. He wrote, in this connection, that normal growth was taking place at the Belgrano church with forty-eight enrolled in the primary class. The Bible

[7]C. Manly Morton, *World Call,* Nov., 1921, p. 41. Used by permission.

school had been organized. Mr. Morton wrote, "I am also organizing a class for the teachers and officers, to meet one night in the week. In this class we will study Bible School methods and plans for one-half hour, and have a general Bible study during the rest of the meeting. We have organized the Men's Bible Class, and are planning to organize a Young Men's Debating Club for one night during the week. There is a great wide field here, which has great promise. It responds to effort, too."[8] Other phases of the educational program, as well as work with the women and children, were carried on by Mrs. Morton.

However, the actual program did not reveal in an adequate way the spiritual tone and the creative atmosphere of the Belgrano church and the work of the Argentine Mission during this decade. During a half century, no other congregation of the Disciples in Argentina has led into Christian service such a large group of young men and young women as did the Belgrano congregation within this period. Mention only can be made of some of these persons. Srta. Elena Colmegna had already become a Christian worker by 1916. She later married Silvio Azzati, Disciple, who grew up in a parsonage, the son of a pioneer Methodist pastor. Others who were members of the Belgrano church and entered Christian service were: Jorgelina Lozada, Feliciano A. Sarli, Clelia Porri Sarli, Manuel Blanco, Federico de Luque, Antonio Navarrette, Antonio de Césare, and Fernando Salem. Four of these persons have continued with Disciples churches in

---

[8]*Missionary Tidings*, Jan., 1918, p. 350.

Argentina either as pastors or as pastors' wives. Also, young people who were converted during this time are laymen and laywomen active in the Belgrano, Saavedra, Colegiales, and Villa Mitre churches.

Srta. Jorgelina Lozada, one of the group, tells how she and her family were won to the Belgrano church. When she was ten or eleven years of age her parents owned a small business not far from the church in Belgrano. In telling her story she says,

One day a young man of Italian birth who was distributing Evangelical literature from house to house came to our home and invited us to church. My mother, whose background was English Protestant, promised to send us children to the Sunday school. My brother and I went the next Sunday and it was an unforgettable experience. The missionaries, Mr. and Mrs. Morton and Mr. and Mrs. Reavis, received us with such attention and affection that we promised to return the next Sunday. We looked forward with expectation as the Sunday school was for us a great event. Our world began to expand and we were happy to have new friends. My parents were very anxious about our education and cautious as to our acquaintances. We were only permitted to go away from home to attend Sunday school and we were very happy with our friends there. Soon my parents began attending church services.

Later my sister and I along with twelve other girls of our age from about fourteen to sixteen made the confession of faith. We were all baptized on Easter Day. It was an occasion which impressed me deeply.

Later the time came for me to decide about my education and future work. I desired to work like the missionaries were doing. Some of them had influenced me profoundly—Miss Zona Smith, Mr. and Mrs. Lemmon and my Sunday school teacher Elena Colmegna, now Sra. Azzati—and I wished also to enter Christian service and work through the church. My parents were not interested in my getting an education that would take me away from home. My father, of Spanish descent, was very conservative about the education of girls, believing it would be unwise for them to leave home. However, when later I desired to enter the Women's Training School, he did not object as he had high respect for and confidence in the director, Miss Zona Smith. So my first experience of being away from home was when, at the age of seventeen, I entered the Training School as a boarding student. This was a new venture in my life. The career which I thus chose has opened many avenues of service and has challenged me to greater endeavor, resulting in an increased interest in the movement for unity and brotherhood which characterize the communion with which I had my first contact and my first spiritual awakening.

My parents and my brothers and sister all united with the church and took part in the work in one form or another. As I write this at a later date, I rejoice that my brothers—now fathers with children—continue loyal to the church and serve in various ways as volunteer workers for the extension of the Kingdom of Christ.[9]

The consecrated effort in building up the congregation of the Disciples and the outreach in the establishment of preaching points during those years was commendable. Yet the more creative genius of the Disciples of Christ in their Argentine Mission work was in the formulation of a working plan for the expanding program of their work in the River Plate Republics. The framework in which this program evolved was in comity as regards territory. Comity meant that responsibility for mission work would be divided on the basis of territory by mutual agreement among mission boards working in a specific area. For a clearer understanding of the background and the cooperative phase of the work, it is important to review the findings of the 1916 Panama Congress on Christian Work. This Congress had awakened in Disciple missionaries a new outlook and an enlarged vision. C. Manly Morton, writing at the end of 1917, said, "Of course, the work of evangelization must not be forgotten, but a program that is broader than has

[9]A personal statement by Srta. Lozada in 1954. Translation by J. D. Montgomery.

ever been laid out for any Latin-American field must be launched if we would take advantage of the greatest opportunities in this field.''[10]

The above statement reflects the attitude and outlook of Disciple missionaries who attended the Congress on Christian Work in Latin America. The entire group of Disciple missionaries in Argentina shared this desire to launch a more comprehensive program of mission work. This broader program was envisioned to include strategic educational work, the preparation of a better-trained national ministry, the betterment of social standards through the education of women, the production of more adequate literature, and an aggressive program of evangelization. Cooperation with other religious bodies was believed to open the way to achieve more effectively much of this program. In the study on ''The Cooperative Task'' one of the underlying principles was stated in the following words:

There is some awakening to the fact that the needs of the people religiously have not been met. Numerous little groups of the people are anxiously waiting for evangelical shepherds whose lives have proven them messengers of the living Christ. This field is absolutely open for evangelical work in all parts, provided it is carried on with sufficient means and in a sufficiently dignified way to demand respect, but the work must be of an increasingly higher grade, more thoroughly educational and scientific, and with churches and schools of adequate importance and equipment to command respect in lands where public buildings are always noteworthy. On the other hand the growth of indifference and irreligion has been so rapid that there is a large class of the more highly educated people entirely inaccessible to the gospel message under present conditions.[11]

These considerations became the basis of careful study as to where the major emphasis should be

---

[10]*Missionary Tidings*, Jan., 1918, p. 350.
[11]Panama Congress, 1916, *op. cit.*, I, 137.

placed in the future program of the Disciples of Christ. The Argentine Mission, along with the board in the U.S.A., weighed carefully the many factors which enter into the planning of such a program. Out of the deliberations there emerged the conviction that the most effective program and the most lasting contribution in the building of Christ's kingdom in Latin America would be through a plan of cooperation with other Protestant communions of like faith and of similar outlook.

Cooperation had been basic to the whole concept in the planning of the Congress on Christian Work in Latin America. While Latin America was omitted from the deliberations of the World Missionary Conference at Edinburgh in 1910, yet it was during this conference that a group of missionaries from Latin America assembled one noon at luncheon to discuss their concern for the needs of Latin America and the great opportunities for the Protestant Church in that field.

As a next step in this development a meeting was held in New York in 1913 at which time a committee was appointed to study the whole matter of a more concerted approach to Protestant mission work in Latin America. This committee was designated the Committee on Cooperation in Latin America. Another meeting was held in the mission room of the Foreign Christian Missionary Society in Cincinnati in June, 1914.[12] As a result of these interdenominational conferences the idea germinated which later flowered in the Congress on Christian Work in Panama. As the newly formed Com-

[12]Stephen J. Corey, *Fifty Years of Attack and Controversy* (St. Louis: The Bethany Press, 1953), p. 57.

mittee on Cooperation in Latin America began to
search for a strong missionary in Latin America to
serve as executive secretary they chose Samuel Guy
Inman who had served for a number of years as a
missionary of the Disciples of Christ in Mexico.
The Christian Woman's Board of Missions under
which Dr. Inman worked granted the request that
he be released for this position, and almost immediately he became active as the executive of this
committee. During 1914, while visiting mission
fields of the Disciples of Christ in Latin America,
Dr. Inman had opportunity to confer with our missionaries in Argentina. Following the Congress in
Panama, regional conferences were held in various
parts of Latin America. Along with Dr. and Mrs.
Charles T. Paul of the College of Missions and Dr.
C. C. Morrison, editor of *The Christian Century,*
all Disciples of Christ, Dr. Inman again visited
Argentina in 1916 and was a member of the regional
conference held in the River Plate Republics.

From the beginning the Disciples shared in the
planning of the Congress in Panama and their representatives entered fully into the deliberations. In
this way the Mission in Argentina had full advantage of the work and findings of this Congress. The
missionaries were ready to profit by them.

The concept of cooperation included comity as
related to territory as well as to institutions and
projects of common purpose and concern. Thus the
Disciples entered into agreements concerning territorial responsibility for parts of Argentina and
for the Republic of Paraguay. In like manner the
Disciples agreed to participate in cooperative enterprises of both educational and evangelistic charac-

ter. First was the comity agreement as regards
territory. This was principally with the Methodist
Mission, as other Protestant bodies in Argentina—
including the Southern Baptists, the Plymouth
Brethren, the Lutherans, the Evangelical Union, the
Waldensians, the Christian and Missionary Alliance,
the Scots Presbyterians—were not ready to participate, although with few exceptions they respected
the spirit of comity.

In 1918, as an outcome of these commitments, the
Disciples accepted the responsibility for the Republic of Paraguay and the Provinces of Entre Ríos
and Corrientes and the Territory of Misiones in
northern Argentina along with work in the city of
Buenos Aires. The Methodists previously had
worked in Paraguay but agreed to concede this
territory to the Disciples. Also, the Methodists
agreed to turn over their churches in the Provinces
of northern Argentina as soon as the Disciples
might be able to enter this field. The Disciples were
ready almost immediately to enter Paraguay, but
were unable to enter the Provinces. So the comity
agreement with the Methodists was never fully
carried out and the Methodists are still in northern
Argentina.

The second phase of the formulation of mission
policy for the Disciples in Argentina was their participation in cooperative projects of missionary endeavor. This brought them early in this decade,
1916-1926, into cooperation in educational institutions and in planning with other missions regarding
matters of common interests and concern for mission work in its larger outreach.

Almost immediately following the Panama Congress, the Disciples entered into a cooperative venture with the Methodists in the training of young ministerial students. The training of young men for the ministry is one of the first concerns of the "younger churches" (congregations on mission fields) and is of prime importance everywhere. It is to the credit of the Disciple Mission in Buenos Aires that within ten years after it began work in the River Plate countries, it was considering ways of recruiting and training young men for the national ministry.

What is now the Union Theological Seminary in Buenos Aires was begun when the Methodist Church in cooperation with the Waldensians started a theological school for the training of ministers in 1884. This later passed to the Methodists exclusively and was conducted by them. In 1916 a Disciple student, Manuel Blanco, found his way into the Methodist seminary in Buenos Aires. The following year steps were taken for a fuller cooperation on the part of the two bodies and Tolbert F. Reavis became a member of the Seminary faculty.[13] In 1918 there were six Disciple students and seven Methodists—perhaps the nearest approach to equality in the number of students ever reached. The Disciple students that year were Manuel Blanco, Rafael Galizia, Antonio de Césare, Antonio Navarrette, Fernando Salem, and Federico de Luque. However, the interdenominational character of the Seminary was not dependent upon an equal number of students from each of the respective cooperating bodies. "At the end of 1918 the president of the Seminary, who

[13]*Missionary Tidings,* July, 1917, p. 91.

was then a Methodist, reported to his Conference that 'the representatives of the two churches have worked in the most perfect harmony, while at the same time there has been the frankest possible expression of doctrinal convictions.' "[14] The teaching, on the whole, in this union institution has not placed emphasis on denominational differences, and the students have been given special instruction in denominational teachings by their own professors. This policy has been followed across the years and in only one instance, to be explained below, were there serious differences of opinion which threatened the cooperative enterprise.

This cooperative work in the Seminary progressed successfully. Other Disciple missionaries who served on the faculty during the early years of this cooperation were C. Manly Morton, Robert B. Lemmon, Charles A. Vannoy, and Abner Johnson. In 1922 Dr. Vannoy became president of the Seminary for two years, being the first Disciple to occupy this position. Tolbert F. Reavis and Abner Johnson of the Disciple Mission taught classes. In 1920 Ambrosio L. Muñiz of the Disciples enrolled as a student; two years later Feliciano A. Sarli enrolled and in 1923 Silvio Azzati entered.

In 1923 differences of opinion over administrative phases of work between Methodists and Disciples led to the withdrawal of the Disciples from the Seminary. A training school for Disciple ministerial students was subsequently established in the Belgrano church building on Cramer Street. This

[14]B. Foster Stockwell, *River Plate Reflections* [June], 1947, pp. [12 f.].

separation was of brief duration, as the two bodies united again in 1925 and the cooperation has continued unbroken since that date.

A more extensive cooperative effort was undertaken when the Disciple Mission joined with the Methodists in the educational program of *Colegio* Ward (then *Colegio Americano;* changed to *Colegio* Ward in 1928).[15] This institution had been started in 1913 by the Methodists. In July, 1917, representatives of the two missions held two meetings at which the proposal for this interdenominational school was studied. Disciples present at these meetings were Samuel Guy Inman, Mr. and Mrs. Tolbert F. Reavis, Mr. and Mrs. C. Manly Morton, and Miss Clara Ida Hill.[16] As a result, a resolution that the two Missions cooperate in the support and development of an institution of learning was approved in 1917 by the home boards (Disciples and Methodists). This was the beginning of a cooperative educational project which has continued without interruption across the years and has won prestige among the educational institutions in the Argentine Republic. The institution is of secondary rather than college rank, as the name might be interpreted to imply.

Among Disciples missionaries who taught in the school during this decade were: Tolbert F. Reavis, Robert B. Lemmon, Samuel S. McWilliams, Alice S.

[15]*Colegio* Ward is named in memory of Mrs. Nancy Gracey Ward (Methodist) of New York City. Her son, George S. Ward, was visiting Buenos Aires, Argentina, at the time of his mother's death in 1913. At that time, he made a gift in honor of his mother for the founding of *Colegio Americano.*

[16]Miss Hill was a Disciple missionary in Mexico during 1912-1913. When compelled to leave Mexico because of revolutionary activities in 1913, she assisted in starting the Mexican Christian Institute in San Antonio, Texas. In 1917, she visited her sister in Buenos Aires and while there, she taught one year in the primary department of the American Division of *Colegio* Ward.

McWilliams, Miss Mary Irene Orvis, Miss Clara Hill, and Howard T. Holroyd.

During this same period there had developed the idea that a school should be organized for the training of young women for Christian service as directors of religious education and as pastors' helpers. In 1922, a dream of Miss Zona Smith came true when she, together with Bishop and Mrs. William F. Oldham of the Methodist Church, secured the approval of their respective mission boards and founded the Women's Training School in Buenos Aires, called the *Instituto Modelo de Obreras Christianas*. Miss Zona Smith was the first director of this Women's Training School, which met favor among the Disciple and Methodist Churches. In 1924 Miss Ruth E. Fish became the director, which place she filled with credit until her return to the United States in 1931. During these early years the Training School made a good beginning.

It is not probable that an interdenominational school of this kind would be in existence had the Disciples not joined with the Methodists in creating it. It has become well established and there is a growing interest in the summer school and regular year courses. Perhaps it is superfluous to mention here the conviction on the part of a few Disciples of the urgent need for the establishment of this institution and the deep interest and joy in its progress and the great desire that it shall always be of ideal service to the Churches through the training of consecrated young women. There is no better testimony needed today for the school than the service rendered by the three young women who were trained in the school: Máxima Villalba, Italina Azzati and Jorgelina Lozada.[17]

The first of the three named was a Methodist. Srta. Italina Azzati served with the Disciples until her marriage when she moved to Rosario and became a

[17]From an unpublished address given by Miss Zona Smith in 1927.

member of the Methodist Church as the Disciples have no work in that city. Srta. Jorgelina Lozada found her place as a worker of the Disciples of Christ and has continued her ministry with Disciple churches and interdenominational work.

Perhaps no vision of the Disciples during this period of their work in Argentina was more forward-looking than their share in the initiation of cooperative work among the women of the Evangelical churches. In September, 1915, Mrs. Tolbert F. Reavis and Miss Zona Smith were invited by Mrs. F. B. Strachan of the Evangelical Union, along with a few other missionaries, to attend a meeting in Tandil to consider the formation of a society for Evangelical women of the whole republic. Societies of Evangelical women had already been formed in towns near Tandil.

The occasion of this meeting was a women's convention which lasted for a week. As a part of the convention, meetings were held with representative women from different communions to consider the possibility of a national organization of Evangelical women. Mrs. Strachan and those in attendance at the convention were united in believing that a national organization of women would be advisable and it was decided to continue studying the matter. This was the beginning of what developed into an effective society of Evangelical women.

In 1916 the second convention of Evangelical women was held in Buenos Aires. In May, 1917, the third convention was held in the First Methodist Church in Buenos Aires, at which time the *Liga*

Nacional de Mujeres Evangélicas (National—later Argentine—League of Evangelical Women) was organized. In May, 1918, Miss Zona Smith, a Disciple, was appointed editor of the monthly bulletin, and in August of the same year she was made executive secretary of the organization, a position which she filled with distinction for many years. She remained editor of the bulletin until her death in 1952. Since its organization in 1917, the League has had a continuous history, and no one deserves more credit for its success than Miss Zona Smith, who gave to it her efficient service and her unfaltering faith.

This venture in the cooperative work of Evangelical women is another example of the creative insights of this decade. By 1926 the membership in the League had grown to 900. In the governing board there were eight Evangelical denominations and organizations represented, and in the whole membership fourteen. The organization and nurture of this interdenominational society of Evangelical women was not easy, but it was tremendously inspiring. Writing in 1927, Miss Smith not only reveals the part which the Disciples had in the formation and development of this cooperative project, but also the aspirations and hopes for its future development:

If there was some fear in the earlier days that a women's organization would not be helpful to the Church, we believe that fear has been dispelled and there is a growing recognition not only of the League, but also of woman's place in all the life of the Church. Perhaps it would not be becoming to say just how significant a part we believe the Disciples have had in this work, but we can say that if the impossible thing could happen that this League should cease to exist today or tomorrow, we would be justified in saying

from the depths of our hearts: ''Thank God that the Disciples were
here and could lend support these twelve years to this women's
movement.''[18]

The Congress on Christian Work in South America met in Montevideo, Uruguay, in 1925. This Congress made a study of mission work in Latin America, including a survey of the work being done, an
examination of the needs in the various fields, and
an evaluation of the program which was in operation. Dr. Stephen J. Corey, Miss Lela E. Taylor,
Mr. and Mrs. R. A. Doan, and E. M. Bowman, all
Disciples of Christ from the United States, attended
this conference. Their visit to South America was
a part of a world survey of the causes of the Disciples of Christ. Following their visit, it was decided to make a more detailed study of the work of
the Disciple mission stations in Argentina and Paraguay. Samuel S. McWilliams, who was on furlough,
returned to supervise this study.

The report appeared in the survey of Disciple
fields published in 1928 as *Survey of Service*. This
was a careful and thorough survey, and became the
basis of further study of the work in Argentina. As
a part of this study the question was raised as to
whether the Disciples should withdraw from Argentina and concentrate their efforts in Paraguay.
There were supporters on both sides of the question.
Due to its wide implications, the matter was placed
in the hands of a committee of the International
Convention of Disciples of Christ, mostly of persons
unfamiliar with the field, and the matter was under
study for too long a time for the good of the work.

[18]*Ibid.*

The committee reported to the International Convention held in Wichita, Kansas, in 1931, when it was finally voted to continue the Disciple Mission in Argentina. This delay in reaching a decision on such a vital issue cooled much of the enthusiasm which characterized the Mission a decade earlier.

An unfortunate handicap to the healthy development of the Disciple Mission in Argentina was the rapid change of personnel during this decade. With the opening of work in Paraguay, Mr. and Mrs. Morton were transferred to Asunción in October, 1918, after two years in Argentina. Mr. and Mrs. Lemmon on returning from furlough in 1924, after one term of service in Argentina, were sent to Asunción. Mr. and Mrs. Abner Johnson after two years in Argentina retired from work and returned home due to his health. Mr. and Mrs. McWilliams went on furlough in 1924, at the end of one term, and were sent to Mexico for one term before returning to Argentina. In 1925, Mr. and Mrs. Tolbert F. Reavis with their four children, after twelve years in Argentina, returned to the United States on furlough and later resigned from mission work.[19]

This history would be unfair to the actual situation of the Disciple Mission in Argentina during 1916-1926 if the impression were left that visions and dreams were transformed into policy and program without struggle and tension. Human organizations and institutions are similar to the great edi-

[19]After returning to the United States, Mr. Reavis became associate professor of Spanish at Butler University in Indianapolis and in 1928 was appointed head of the Department of Sociology. In 1928, Indiana University conferred on Mr. Reavis the Ph.D. degree and in the same year he received the LL.D. from Culver-Stockton College. Mrs. Reavis died in 1935, and following an illness Dr. Reavis taught at the Laconia High School and later in Midway Junior College at Midway, Kentucky. After retirement, he did ad-interim work as pastor in different churches.

fice which relies upon a steel framework for its skel-
eton and supporting structure. This framework and
structure must be wrought out of undeveloped materials and refined into a carefully planned, strong,
durable edifice. In somewhat like manner it takes
time for a newly trained staff of an organization
to season and to gain perspective. The rapidity
with which events moved during this decade did not
allow time for newly enlisted and recently trained
personnel to mature in experience and ripen in
loyalty in a way comparable to the casting of steel
which goes into the structure of a great edifice.

During the early years of the Argentine Mission,
the program evolved slowly and policy was simple.
Then came the enlarged program following 1916
which led into new endeavors and more complexity
in policy of work and in administration. The enthusiasm of this expanding program gave impetus
to outreach and to additional planning. It was
simpler, however, to formulate Mission policy than
to administer this policy in the details of daily work.
The practical issues of daily activities involved a
program where persons with their likes and dis-
likes, their aspirations and their convictions were
involved. It was soon evident that the new policy
would need to wrestle with unforeseen issues which
would tax its strength to the maximum in the future.

In the early 1920's, this complexity of policy became further involved, as the Mission wrestled with
the delicate problem as to the place and responsibility of national workers. How were they to share
in the planning and the administration of the Mission, and particularly in the administration of the

work of the churches? This question of administration and of responsibility became an issue when Tolbert F. Reavis left the work in 1925 and the pastorate of the Belgrano church became vacant. Sr. Rafael Galizia, a national, was named by the Mission to succeed Mr. Reavis as pastor of the Belgrano church. This choice lacked full support of other Disciple national ministers, and tensions arose within the group of nationals which were much more pointed than when a missionary held this pastorate. The repercusions of this struggle were in evidence for a number of years.

Also, the Mission had now developed to the place where doctrinal issues were involved. Doctrinal differences tended to exaggerate the tensions among national workers and increased the cleavage between some of the missionaries and Argentine Disciple ministers. The Congress on Christian Work held in Montevideo in 1925 had impressed some of the Disciple Argentine ministers that undue emphasis was being placed on the liberal tenets of the Christian faith. As is usually the case, it is difficult to separate the tensions over administrative policy from difference as to faith and doctrine. However, as an outcome of these tensions, from the doctrinal as well as the administrative angle, two national ministers withdrew from the Disciples and found their allegiance within the ministry of Southern Baptist churches. Sr. Rafael Galizia resigned from the pastorate of the Belgrano church at the end of 1925, after one year of service, and accepted the ministry of the Baptist church in the city of Corrientes. At the same time Sr. Blas A. Maradei, pastor of the church on Rivera Street, withdrew from the Disciples and took his congregation with him, becoming affiliated with the Baptist Convention in Argentina, with which both he and the congregation had been associated before coming to the Disciples some ten years earlier.

During this decade the Disciple Mission published the magazine *El Discípulo (The Disciple)* which followed the publication by Mr. Burner, *La Luz y la Verdad.* Later *El Discípulo* was changed to *El Mensajero (The Messenger)* which has continued as the organ of the Disciple Churches in Argentina. In 1925 the Disciple Mission in Buenos Aires published in Spanish a booklet entitled *Compendio de la Historia de los Discípulos Tomás and Alejandro Campbell.* This was composed of sections taken from the book by Archibald McLean entitled *Thomas and Alexander Campbell* (Cincinnati, 1910). The Spanish edition was translated and published by Mr. Reavis and Sr. Salem.

In a review of the work of the Disciple Mission in Argentina during the years 1916-1926, many things stand out which are worthy of commendation. The long-range planning of entering into cooperative phases of mission work as well as the decision to establish mission work in Paraguay with an educational rather than an evangelistic emphasis has met the test of three and one-half decades of constructive Christian service and Kingdom building. Yet with the policy which was formulated, limitations were placed upon the Mission in its program of evangelization. The responsibilities assumed by the Disciples in the educational program in Paraguay and their commitments in the union projects in Argentina placed a heavy load upon both the budget and the personnel. This load proved to be more than the Mission was able to carry and so the evangelistic program as it had been originally outlined became impossible. Thus the plan to extend work north of Buenos Aires into the Provinces of Entre Ríos and Corrientes and the territory of Missiones was not realized.

Writing from Buenos Aires in 1919, Robert B. Lemmon graphically states the situation in the following way:

> . . . In an instant you will see our position here, one man and three women to do the work that demands twelve people as the minimum. Mr. and Mrs. Reavis have had about seven years' experience of lack of workers, with its consequent ''helpless'' feeling. I don't think it is biblical to have more than seven years of famine, so we are hoping for better times. We hope you will insist on as many workers as possible, as soon as possible. ''Compel them to come.''[20]

Two tendencies lead in opposite directions as one attempts to record the events of the Disciple Mission in Argentina during this decade. One tendency is to record only what is commendable and constructive. The other is to become unduly pessimistic. As one who had a vital share in the shaping of the history of the Mission during the two decades following the one under consideration, the writer, who arrived on the field in March, 1926, shares with many others the view that the policy adopted during these years will increasingly show the wisdom of those who had part in its making. Certainly the task was not an easy one and at many times the program appeared to be ill defined.

However, as a fair evaluation would seem to indicate, the policy followed in Buenos Aires embodies

[20]*World Call,* Sept., 1919, p. 43.

three constructive and farsighted elements: (1) the cooperative work in the Seminary, *Colegio* Ward, the Women's Training School, and the Argentine League of Evangelical Women, placed before Christians in Argentina a living example of cooperative effort and constructive achievement; (2) the standard of education in these schools was at a higher level than could have been true with each communion working separately; and (3) the influence of the Disciples' plea for unity was greatly multiplied by means of these practical demonstrations. Perhaps the conclusions of Miss Zona Smith writing from Argentina will help readers assess the work of the Mission during these years:

The Disciples have stood by the job in season and out of season, through difficulties too numerous to mention, the seed sowing continuing year in and year out, and in spite of all the imperfections and mistakes of laymen and missionaries and the strong opposition of the enemy of all righteousness, God's Spirit did work and the Church has been established. . . . Sometimes the uplift comes so slowly that we can see progress only with the eye of faith. We are not yet convinced that the neediest fields are where the people respond most readily to the gospel call. . . . It is a great satisfaction to me that God directed my steps to Argentina and that since 1910 it has been my privilege to have a small part in this tragic struggle. Our evangelistic work is the best today that it has ever been, and the example of persistent effort, already mentioned . . ., is of untold value to our Latin-American Christians. . . . These last two years there has come to me a far better insight than ever before into what the missionary task really is and at what we are really working. The enterprise is so much bigger and so much more interesting than the necessary and essential ploughing of the furrows day by day. And whether we would have it so or not, ours is a part of the whole evangelical work of the community and of Argentina, of Paraguay, and of the whole Continent.[21]

[21]Smith, *op. cit.*, (1927).

Chapter VI

Budgets Talk
and Responsibilities Shift
1926-1936

The third decade of mission work in Argentina by the Disciples of Christ may rightly be called the period in which the missionaries decreased and the responsibility of the national workers increased. In 1927 there were eleven missionaries on the field; ten years later there were only four. After almost twenty years of experience in this field, J. D. Montgomery wrote:

As one looks back to the work of our churches in Argentina during the years from 1926-1936, many memories clamor for expression. Acquaintances which flowered into lifelong friendships appeal for mention and recognition. Loyalty and confidence, trust and faithfulness were built into comradeship which only a poet could weave into words. These cords of comradeship and brotherhood came out of the common task of building a church program in an environment which tested the walls of the structure at every stage of development. There were losses as well as gains, personality was weighed against personality, ideas clashed with ideas—it was a youthful and vigorous atmosphere—basic structures were in the building and tough timber was an essential element to make for permanency.[1]

Events moved rapidly in Argentina from 1926 to 1936; the repercussions of an economic world upheaval; a national political revolution; a Roman Catholic Eucharistic Congress held in Buenos Aires; a cut in missionary budget with subsequent with-

---

[1]From a statement made by J. D. Montgomery in 1947.

drawal of missionaries from the field; a new location for Ward School; the first youth conference of
Evangelical Churches; the divisive effects of religious controversy; the organization of a Disciple
Council of Churches; and the establishment of a
Union Bookstore. These all added variety to the
missionary task, placing new strains upon the young
churches as they were struggling to establish themselves in the community and within the larger body
of Christians.

Constructive gains, disappointments, and retrenchments were all ingredients in building
Christ's Kingdom in Argentina. Expansion into
new fields of evangelization were meager. Yet foundations for future work were laid which were constructive and positive. Increasingly the responsibility of administration, of support, and of propagation was shifted from missionaries to national workers and Argentine churches. The basic principles
of Christian stewardship were being implanted. Cooperative aspects of Christian work were more
closely cemented and this ten-year period showed
constructive achievements.

The study of the work of Disciple mission stations
in Argentina and Paraguay as part of the *Survey
of Service* of Disciple Missions (mentioned in the
previous chapter) had a negative effect upon the
evangelistic outreach of the churches in Argentina.
This study raised the question as to whether Disciples should continue in Argentina and thus fore-
stalled the expansion of evangelistic work during
the first half of this decade. When the final decision
was voted at the International Convention in Wichita, Kansas, in 1931, that the Disciple Mission in

Argentina be continued, the economic depression had forced cuts in mission budgets which again delayed expansion.

The rapid change of Disciple missionary personnel which characterized the previous decade continued through this ten-year period. Lora Aletta Garrett, born in Shelbyville, Missouri, arrived in Buenos Aires, August 4, 1925. Three days later she started teaching in the American high school division of *Colegio* Ward. She served as teacher of English and as high school principal until the end of the school year in 1930. She then taught one year at *Colegio Internacional* in Paraguay before going on furlough. In February, 1933, she returned to the American School in Buenos Aires, where she served one year as a contract teacher. On December 12 of that year she was married in La Paz, Bolivia, to Gustav Mehlis, a businessman. They have two sons.

J. Dexter and Anna Kate Montgomery with their daughter, Anita, joined the Disciple Mission in Buenos Aires in March, 1926. Both natives of Virginia, they had served one term in the Disciple Mission in Puerto Rico, where Anita was born, before going to Argentina. Mr. Montgomery became pastor of the Belgrano church and was the Disciple representative on the faculty of the Union Theological Seminary, serving also as vice-director of that institution. Mrs. Montgomery was active in the educational program of the women's work in Disciple churches and in the Argentine League of Evangelical Women.

Howard T. and Leona McMahon Holroyd with their three children, Janet, John, and David, returned to the United States on furlough in 1928, having spent one term as Disciple representatives in *Colegio* Ward.   In the same year Hugh J. and Winifred W. Williams, who had worked for two years with the Disciple Mission in Asunción, Paraguay, were transferred to Buenos Aires to take the place left vacant by the Holroyds at *Colegio* Ward. He was born in Pennsylvania and she in Iowa. Winifred had spent seven years of her life as a child in the Philippine Islands where her parents were Disciple missionaries.   During their first year in Buenos Aires, Mrs. Williams served as vice-principal and teacher in the Women's Training School.

Normal B. and Mae Yoho Ward, both of West Virginia, arrived in Buenos Aires in the fall of 1928.   During their five years in Buenos Aires, the Wards entered widely into the work of the Mission. With his training and interest in recreation, Mr. Ward made a constructive contribution in the preparation of a book of games in Spanish.   Their daughter, Dee Yoho, died in her native Buenos Aires at the age of two.   Mr. and Mrs. Ward with their son, Don Jeff, born in Argentina, returned to the United States on furlough in March, 1934, and later took up pastoral work in Ohio.

At the end of 1930, Ruth E. Fish, after eight years as principal of the Women's Training School, resigned from the Disciple Mission in Argentina. She returned to her home in California to be with her mother, who was in poor health.   There she again entered the teaching profession.   Dr. Rhoda

Edmeston, Methodist, succeeded Miss Fish as principal of the Training School. In July, 1931, Ina
Lee Foster was appointed to the Disciple Argentine
Mission in Buenos Aires where she was vice-principal and teacher at the Training School. Before
her appointment to the Argentine Mission, Miss
Foster had served for five years under the Woman's
Foreign Missionary Society of the Methodist
Church, in Crandon Institute, an outstanding school
for girls in Montevideo, Uruguay. At the end of
1932 she received word that her work in Argentina
would close due to budget reductions.

In March, 1931, Mr. and Mrs. Montgomery left on
furlough and returned to the United States by way
of Europe. Due to drastic reductions in the budget,
they remained in the homeland until March, 1934.
Upon returning to Buenos Aires, he again resumed
his responsibilities in the Union Theological Seminary, carried administrative responsibilities as
member of the Disciple Mission, and became pastor
of the Colegiales church.

At the end of 1930, Mr. and Mrs. Samuel S. Mc-
Williams, after four years of service with the Disciple Mission in Mexico, returned to the Disciple
Argentine Mission and their work in *Colegio* Ward,
the field of their first endeavor and of their first
love.

The Central Council of Disciple Churches was organized in 1929 with the national workers, the missionaries, and two elected laymen as members. This
was the first formal attempt to include Argentinians
in the administration of the church work. The purpose of the Council was to guide the work of the
Disciple churches. During the years it has de-

veloped into an efficient organization and has done systematic and forward-looking planning. The first convention of Disciple churches in Argentina was held in January, 1929, and was of an inspirational and educational character. During its early history the convention met only periodically, but later was established as an annual convention. It is a delegated convention. An effective program is planned each year, with prominent speakers invited from other communions, as well as messages by leading Disciple ministers and lay members. In addition to the worship and inspirational features, time is provided for educational subjects. In its business sessions reports are made for the various congregations and recommendations are voted looking toward the improvement and expansion of the church work. As a part of the convention business, the lay representatives are elected to the Central Council.

Colegiales was the second congregation of the Disciples permanently established in Buenos Aires. Since 1910 this congregation had conducted its worship and other activities in rented buildings. Lots were purchased in 1918 on the corner of Federico Lacroze and Zapiola Streets, but funds were not available for a church building until 1930. On August 17 of that year the cornerstone was laid and the new building was dedicated in March, 1931.

This building not only gave the congregation an adequate building, but it also contributed to the beauty of architecture among Protestant churches in Argentina. This became a positive gain as the Protestant movement was growing in the Republic and more attractive and better-equipped church

buildings gave permanence and prestige to its development. Sr. Silvio Azzati was pastor of the
Colegiales congregation for some eight years. At
the close of his pastorate in 1933, N. B. Ward became pastor for one year. Following him, J. D.
Montgomery served as pastor until 1943.

A movement which grew in importance both in
Disciple churches and interdenominationally was
the Daily Vacation Church School started and developed in the Belgrano church in this decade.

The Disciples of Christ were among the pioneers
in admitting women of the Protestant churches to
the Christian ministry. Srta. Jorgelina Lózada, a
Disciple, was the first woman to serve as the pastor
of an Evangelical church in the River Plate region.
Her love for the church, her high esteem for the
ministry, her devoted service, and her loyalty to the
cause of Christ won for Srta. Lozada recognition
and advancement. As she grew and developed in
the work, it was felt that she should be ordained as
a Christian worker. The service of ordination was
held in her home church in Belgrano in 1930 when
she was ordained as a home missionary. This pio-
neering venture in the recognition of womanhood in
Christian service has been justified by subsequent
events and achievements.

Perhaps no experience related to the missionary
program of the church causes more yearning of
soul or searching of heart than when missionaries
who have been tried and found faithful must be recalled from the field because of cuts in missionary
budgets. This was the issue which faced the executives of The United Christian Missionary Society
during the economic depression of the 1930's.

Budgets within the homeland, along with those of all mission fields, received drastic cuts due to the reduced income of the Society. These reduced budgets affected not only the missionaries, but also devoted and consecrated national workers who had dedicated their lives to Christian service. Churches in some cases were closed and work which may not have been well established was abandoned.

The Argentine Mission was affected, in the first place, by the reduction of the missionary staff. In 1933 the United Society found it necessary to retire Miss Zona Smith, to discontinue its financial support to the Women's Training School, and to recall the Disciple representative in that institution,[2] Miss Ina Lee Foster.

This reduced the Disciple missionary staff in Argentina to two couples, the Wards and the Mc-Williamses. Miss Foster accepted a position as science teacher in Santiago College, a girls' school in Chile conducted by the Methodist board, a position which she held until 1935, when she returned to her home in Kentucky to be with her father.

With Miss Zona Smith roots of her affection and commitment had gone much deeper and to eradicate them would have required a terrific pull. She became a part of the staff in Argentina in 1910 and had given faithful and loyal service, endearing herself to members of Disciple churches as well as to a much larger group among other Protestant bodies. Rather than retire she decided to resign from the Mission and to stay on with the interdenominational

---

[2]Cooperation was continued by Disciple missionaries teaching part time until the Training School and the Union Seminary united in 1942.

work which had become the choice of a lifetime service. So without salary from the United Society, using private income, she rented a small apartment and lived simply; she continued her excellent contribution to cooperative missions work in Argentina.

When the cablegram from the United States reached Argentina in 1933, cutting the budget to what seemed an impossible amount, the first reaction was that one church would have to be closed and a worker dropped. At no other time in the history of the Disciple Mission in Argentina had the national workers faced so realistically their responsibility in making decisions in the administration of church work as they did at that moment. After careful study they decided to share the reduction in salaries rather than close one of the churches or ask one of the workers to resign. The Villa Mitre congregation, whose work would be closed, had a meeting and pledged fifty pesos a month toward self-support. It was then voted that the Argentine pastors would accept half salary and find part-time outside work to supplement the amount received from the Mission and from the churches.

This experience revealed something of the character of the Argentine pastors. Srta. Jorgelina Lozada agreed to take charge of the Villa Mitre congregation on the condition that she secure half-time work at the Y.W.C.A. as secretary of the employment bureau. When in 1935 the Y.W.C.A. needed someone to head a new work in Montevideo, she was considered for the place. The general secretary, out of respect for the Disciple Mission, consulted the missionaries about the new offer. It was

Modern Buenos Aires

Right: Belgrano Church,
    1911

Below: Colegiales Church,
    1931

Bottom: Villa Mitre
    Church, 1940

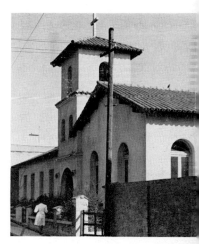

Above: Saavedra Church,
    1950

Right: Resistencia Church,
    1953

Bottom: Beginning of work
    in Barranqueras

Porqueras from Black Star

Disciple pastors and seminary students hold interview at Union Seminary, 1955

Executive Committee of Central Council of Disciple Churches meets in Buenos Aires, 1955

Porqueras from Black Star

Children of Disciple churches in Argentina grow through fellowship and purposeful activities

Faculty and student body of Union Seminary and Women's Training School preceding merger of the two institutions in 1942

Students visiting in front of building erected in 1943, when combined student body had grown to seventy-seven in 1955

Porqueras from Black Star

Students of Colegio Ward in Buenos Aires relaxing on the school grounds between classes, April, 1951. Some boys and girls are in white smocks called "guardapolvos" used to protect clothes

First Evangelical summer youth conference held in Argentina, 1927

Adult-family conference at morning devotions, 1952

Youth conference, one of four interdenominational summer conferences held on Colegio Ward campus in 1954.   Disciple churches
have participated in these conferences since their beginning

felt proper that Srta. Lozada herself should decide, and when the response came it was in keeping
with her temperament—spontaneous, decisive, firm:

> . . . I shall not forget the mild censure with which she even
> chided us missionaries for thinking she might leave her place as a
> pastor of a church. Yes, in the Y.W.C.A. she could do religious
> work, but less effectively than in the church; there she could do real
> service, but without the warmth and sustaining fellowship which the
> church offers; there she could find a wide field of activities, but
> not in keeping with her preparation in the same way as with the
> church. The question was decided and we were thankful. Her
> calling was again vindicated.[3]

One Disciple pastor, Sr. Feliciano A. Sarli, who
was in charge of two churches in Buenos Aires, secured half-time work with a business firm as cashier
and bookkeeper while continuing his work as pastor
on a half-time basis. Another pastor, Sr. A. L.
Muñiz, accepted a reduction in salary but continued
his work with the church. In order to supplement
his meager income his wife found work, for a time,
outside of the home. These examples indicate how
the pastors of Disciple churches and their families
responded during this emergency period of the depression and accepted the responsibility of helping
to maintain the church work.

Issues of another nature became acute during
this ten-year period. Theological controversy,
which was manifest in the previous decade, again
became a divisive force. This time the controversy
was of a different kind. Followers of Spiritualism
began to infiltrate some Disciple congregations.
This became an issue of major importance and it

[3]J. D. Montgomery, *World Call*, March, 1940, p. 35.

became necessary for the Central Council of Disciples Churches to take official action. As a result the pastor of the Colegiales congregation, Silvio Azzati, was appointed to another pastorate. This he was not ready to accept and instead resigned from the Central Council and accepted the pastorate of a non-Disciple congregation. In 1941 he expressed a desire to re-enter work with the Disciples. After careful consideration the Central Council of Disciple Churches appointed him as pastor of the Belgrano church of the Disciples, which position he filled with credit.

In the cooperative work with which the Disciples were affiliated, significant accomplishments were achieved. Among these were developments in work with young people. In 1927 the first Interdenominational Summer Youth Conference initiated by H. P. Hauser, Methodist, and J. D. Montgomery, was held on the newly purchased grounds of *Colegio* Ward. This was a pioneer venture for the Evangelical churches in Argentina. Trained leaders were not available and equipment was very meager. But the movement took root and grew.

During the early 1920's the Argentine Federation of Evangelical Youth was formed in Buenos Aires. The influence of this organization extended beyond Argentina into Uruguay and Chile. The Federation was distinctively religious and at first was simple, but as the organization grew its influence became more extensive. In March, 1927, the Federation began the publication of a monthly magazine, *La Elevación (Elevation)*, which was dedicated to young people of the Evangelical churches as a means of disseminating religious teaching.

Later this organization began religious broadcasts over the radio twice monthly, which were increased until in 1931 broadcasts were given twice weekly. These young people also held annual assemblies, institutes, and special meetings for the enrichment of their members and the propagation of their ideals.

Under the auspices of the Committee on Cooperation in Latin America, E. Stanley Jones, the famous missionary to India, visited Argentina in 1928 and lectured in a number of the larger cities of the Republic. Following his visit George P. Howard, an Argentine pastor of the Methodist Church, was chosen as the evangelist-at-large of the Committee on Cooperation in Latin America. Dr. Howard traveled widely and lectured to large audiences in the leading cities of Latin America and the United States. He became a missionary link of the Pomona, California, First Christian Church. Through the influence of these lecture tours, the gospel message was extended into sections of society, particularly the intellectual class, which the ordinary program of the churches was unable to reach.

The establishment in 1926 of the Union Bookstore, *La Aurora,* in Buenos Aires as an interdenominational venture was auspicious. The enthusiasm of its beginnings was overshadowed by an unduly large overhead. It had a choice location on one of the prominent streets of Buenos Aires. The original stock was not sufficient to carry the outlay for operation and it became necessary to draw on the original investment to care for the deficit. The struggle to keep afloat seemed increasingly impossible and was augmented by the economic depression in the 1930's. So the decision was reached that the Bookstore would of necessity be discontinued. Dr. W. E. Browning, writing in 1934, said:

> The one piece of Cooperative work that, in a way, has been unfortunate, is *La Aurora,* the Union Evangelical bookstore which was established in Buenos Aires, in 1926. Several factors have contributed to what now seems to be the inevitable closing of this business. The first and the principal one, no doubt, is the economic crisis, which has closed many other stores of a similar character. Many families that formerly bought books, now find themselves so financially distressed that the purchase of bread, rather than books, has become a problem. Some clashing of personalities has complicated the situation. And the various evangelical groups have not rallied to the support of their own institution, as was hoped might be the case, but practically abandoned it to its fate as soon as it was launched on the troubled commercial sea of Buenos Aires. . . . It seems necessary to close out the business hoping to realize sufficient to pay the outstanding debts.[4]

Fortunately for the fate of the Union Bookstore, there was unending legal red tape which delayed for many months a final settlement of the business. In the meantime a few interested persons took the initiative in starting a movement to revive interest in the store. This resulted in the postponement of the liquidation and the Bookstore was saved. The stock of books on hand was again put on sale and a more fortunate plan for operating the business reduced expenses. Arrangements were made with the executive secretary of the American Bible Society, Sr. Paul Penzotti, to administer the Union Bookstore along with the Bible Society. From that time the Bookstore began to recoup its lost capital. This plan of administration, together with additional investments by some of the denomina-

---

[4]W. E. Browning, Report of the Executive Secretary of the Committee on Cooperation in the River Plate Republics, October, 1934. Unpublished.

tional groups, particularly the Methodists and the Disciples, helped it to become established on a sound financial basis and its future was assured. It was to become one of the effective cooperative agencies in the River Plate Republics for the production and dissemination of Evangelical literature.

The year 1933 was a significant one for *Colegio* Ward. The school celebrated its twentieth anniversary and dedicated its new buildings which had been constructed on the beautiful campus in Ramos Mejía, a suburb of Buenos Aires. Having maintained through two decades of faithful service a high education standard, the school entered its new property with wide recognition and warm appreciation. The Spanish-speaking section of the school was moved to the present site in Ramos Mejía. The new campus, purchased in 1926, consisted of eighteen acres of land (later increased to thirty acres) previously an elegant homestead. The new buildings, surrounded by trees, shrubs, and flowers, presented a favorable atmosphere for education and character building. Erected on this new property were an administration building, a boys' dormitory, and a dining-hall unit, at the cost of $265,000.

Colegio Ward thus celebrated its twentieth anniversary with a sense of accomplishment. Its scholastic standing was recognized by school authorities and by its patrons. The influence the school exerted beyond its classroom work was indicated in the annual report of the director, Dr. Fred Aden, as follows:

We have had a continual stream of educational authorities and inspectors visiting us during the year. Mr. Ernesto Nelson, a government inspector of secondary schools, has been a valuable friend

of the school, bringing with him on several occasions educational
authorities who spent several hours at the school, having lunch with
the students, the better to understand the work we are doing.[5]

The new location for the Spanish-speaking section
of the school gave room for expansion both in program and in enrollment. The enrollment following
the new location rose to 442 students, an increase of
fifteen per cent over the previous year. Two years
later the student body numbered 600.

The American School division, with its boarding
department, remained in the old property, Rivadavia 6100, with rented annex, until it was moved
to Belgrano, a district within Buenos Aires, in 1941.

Sponsored by the Union Theological Seminary,
and usually held within its walls, the Ministers' Institutes were initiated in 1932. These began with
a small group of ministers, mainly graduates of
the Union Seminary who came together for study,
fellowship, and inspiration. Within a few years
these gatherings became well-organized Ministers'
Institutes in which national ministers and missionaries came together annually to study problems
common to their tasks as Christian workers. Later
twelve to eighteen communions were represented in
these annual gatherings. They have had a wide
and constructive influence. Besides stimulating the
intellectual life of the pastors who attend, they have
enhanced the movement of Christian unity by
strengthening the intellectual and spiritual bases
for cooperation. B. Foster Stockwell, director of

[5]Annual Report, 1933, made to the Board of Managers of *Colegio
Ward* in Buenos Aires.

the Union Theological Seminary, initiated these institutes and has been the moving spirit in promoting them.

When J. D. Montgomery went on furlough in 1931, N. B. Ward took his place as a member of the faculty of the Union Theological Seminary, which place Mr. Ward filled until he left for furlough in 1934. In addition Mr. Ward was named ad-interim director of the Seminary in 1933 when B. Foster Stockwell returned to the United States on furlough and this position he held for one and one-half years. At the same time Mr. and Mrs. Ward lived in the Seminary building and made a home for the Seminary students.

An important event which concerned Disciple churches in Argentina was the World Convention of the World Council of Christian Education and Sunday School Association (formerly the World's Sunday School Association), held in Río de Janeiro, Brazil, July, 1932. There were 1,636 delegates registered from thirty-three countries of the world, coming from every continent. Disciple delegates from Argentina who attended the convention were N. B. Ward and Jorgelina Lozada. Dr. Robert M. Hopkins, a Disciple and secretary of the World's Sunday School Association, visited Buenos Aires as part of his trip to South America in 1930 when making plans for the convention. Following the convention in Río de Janeiro in 1932, Disciple delegates who visited Argentina were: Misses Etta Nunn and May Wilson from Mexico, Dr. Hopkins, Dr. Roger T. Nooe, and Dr. S. Guy Inman from the United States, the latter three being Disciple members of the Board of Trustees of *Colegio* Ward who were present for a special ceremony in connection with the dedication of the new buildings on the Ramos Mejía campus.

The religious event of major importance which took place in Argentina during this decade was the celebration of the thirty-second International Eucharistic Congress by the Roman Catholic Church in 1934. The care with which the preparation and promotion were made, the dramatic nature of the Congress, and the wide participation indicated that trends in Argentina were toward a renewed spiritual emphasis. The principal gatherings of the Congress took place in the beautiful Palermo Park, where arrangements for outdoor services provided accommodations estimated sufficient to seat 200,000. Loud speakers carried the messages within hearing disance of a large part of the entire populace of the city of Buenos Aires. The Congress, without doubt, touched and moved the citizens of the Argentine, and especially of Buenos Aires, as no other religious event in this decade. Representatives of thirty nations participated in the ceremonies.

As one summarizes the happenings which recount the problems, the retrenchments, the struggles, and the achievements of this decade, all is not on the debit side of the ledger. During these ten years, the population of Buenos Aires increased from 2,000,000 to 2,300,000; Disciple-organized churches grew from two to four; local church giving increased annually from $200 to $1,300. *Colegio* Ward expansion included three new buildings on the Ramos Mejía campus. The Union Theological Seminary reorganized its library, added summer and correspondence courses and night classes. The

Union Bookstore showed a steady growth in sales and prestige, rendering increasing service to the Evangelical community by making available good literature in both Spanish and English.

Also, in 1927 the first Young People's Conference (interdenominational) was held at Ramos Mejía, attendance continuing to increase each year thereafter. The Central Council of Disciple Churches, with missionaries, national workers and two laymen, was organized in 1929 and indicated the progress made in delegating responsibility to the Argentine churches and their pastors. The dedication of the new Disciple church building in Colegiales on March 15, 1931, provided inspiration and enthusiasm not only for that congregation but also for other Evangelical churches.

CHAPTER VII

A Decade of Building and Growth

1936-1946

Since the friendly relationships between the governments and the peoples of Argentina and the United States have so often been strained during the last fifty years, it seems fitting that a brief statement be made about the period opening the decade under consideration. Also, it seems well to include some recognition of international concern which came to citizens of Argentina.

At no time during the first half of the twentieth century was there a closer friendship or more cordial diplomatic relationship between the peoples and governments of the United States and the Argentine Republic than was manifested in 1936. This good feeling came as the result of specific achievements among the American nations through the Pan-American Union, but was heightened by the visit of President Franklin D. Roosevelt to the Inter-American Peace Conference held in Buenos Aires. President Roosevelt arrived in Buenos Aires on November 3 and stayed exactly forty-nine hours in Argentina. The popular tribute to him was pronounced by *La Prensa*, the outstanding daily in Buenos Aires, to be "simply magnificent." There was official warmth as well as popular acclaim to the reception given to the President of the United States. Dr. S. Guy Inman, for many years executive secretary of the Committee on Cooperation in Latin America, was an official adviser to the delegation of the United States Government at this Inter-American Peace Conference.

This good feeling had been fostered through a visit to the Argentine Republic by President-elect Herbert Hoover in 1928; through the Pan-American Conference held in Montevideo in 1933 when Secretary of State Cordell Hull headed the United States delegation and plans were approved which implemented the Good Neighbor Policy in inter-American Relations. Good will between the two republics was further enhanced by the Inter-American Peace Conference in Buenos Aires as it worked toward the conclusion of the war between Bolivia and Paraguay.

Argentina was also brought before world opinion by the awarding on November 25, 1936, of the Nobel Peace Prize to Dr. Carlos Saavedra Lamas, who was then minister of Foreign Relations of Argentina. For the first time this brought the coveted prize to the continent of South America. The accomplishments of Dr. Saavedra Lamas as professor and legislator, as well as his efforts in the interest of better international relations, of world social problems, of universal understanding and good will and of anti-war treaties, won for him this merited recognition.

Recognition again came to Argentina during this period with the conferring, on December 19, 1935, of the Cardinal's red cap on the Archbishop of Argentina, Santiago Luis Copello, by Pope Pius XI. This was the first Cardinal in the Roman Catholic Church of Spanish-speaking South America and was a recognition of the growing importance of the Catholic Church in South America and in Argentina. The only other Cardinal in South America was one in Portuguese Brazil.

The change of missionary personnel of the Disciples of Christ in this ten-year period was not so frequent as in previous years. Samuel S. and Alice Sheplee McWilliams continued their services at *Colegio* Ward. When J. Dexter and Anna Kate Montgomery returned to the field in 1934, he became pastor of the Colegiales Church and was again on the faculty of the Union Seminary. In 1935 Mrs. Montgomery was asked to take charge of the boys' boarding department in the American School division of *Colegio* Ward for a year and, as a result, the Montgomerys moved from the Colegiales apartment to the Rivadavia 6100 building. The following year she was named head of the girls' dormitory, which position she held until the American School division was moved to Belgrano in 1939, coinciding with the Montgomerys' going on furlough.

Upon their return to Argentina in 1941, Mrs. Montgomery was put in charge of the boarding department of the Union Theological Seminary, which position, as well as those in the American School division of *Colegio* Ward, she filled with credit. She also taught in the Women's Training School and was assistant treasurer of the League of Evangelical Women. Due to the illness of their daughter, Anita, Mr. and Mrs. Montgomery found it necessary to return to the homeland in January, 1944.

No two missionaries ever worked harder, more wisely, more efficiently, or more lovingly than did the Montgomerys during their twenty-four years of service in Puerto Rico and Argentina and it was with deep heartaches, both on their part and that of the people among whom they had worked that they found it necessary to relinquish their work on the mission field and settle, for a time at least, in the United States.[1]

On reaching the United States, they made their home in Indianapolis, Indiana, and continued with The United Christian Missionary Society, Mr. Montgomery becoming national director of adult work and Christian family life in the department of religious education. As a part of his work as director of Christian family life, Mr. Montgomery attended the Conference on the Church and Marriage, sponsored by the World Council of Churches, held at the Ecumenical Institute near Geneva, Switzerland, in June, 1953.

In September, 1943, George Earle and Margaret Richards Owen, both of Virginia, arrived in Buenos Aires and were named to the faculty of the Union Theological Seminary, succeeding the Montgomerys as Disciple representatives in that institution.

In November, 1943, Paul and Lucy Wade Andress, he a native of Ohio and she from Arkansas, arrived in Buenos Aires and were appointed to the pastorate of the Colegiales church. They had previously spent one term with the Disciple Mission in Paraguay where they worked in *Colegio Internacional.* Before her marriage in 1938 Mrs. Andress had served as a missionary of the Methodist Church, South, for nine years in Brazil.

In January, 1944, Miss Hallie Lemon of Nebraska arrived in Buenos Aires and was assigned to religious education work with the Saavedra church.

[1]*They Went to Latin America* (Indianapolis: The United Christian Missionary Society, 1947), p. 69.

Miss Lemon's experience has been varied and fruitful and she deserves to be considered an international missionary. Before going to Argentina she had spent nine years as a Disciple missionary in Mexico, having gone there in 1920. She then spent two years with the Disciple Mission in Puerto Rico in the early 1930's. After seven years in Argentina she served one year in Paraguay and was later appointed to Mexico for another three-year term.

One of the cherished dreams of the Disciple Mission in Argentina came to fruition in 1944 when a new mission station was opened in the city of Resistencia, National Territory of the Chaco, some 700 miles north of Buenos Aires. It had been a basic part of the Mission policy to open work outside of the Capital of the Argentine Republic, and more than twenty years earlier plans were formulated for establishing churches in the provinces north of Buenos Aires. For two decades this proposal had remained unrealized. In 1941 the Committee on Evangelism of the Disciple Council of Churches in Buenos Aires began a study which resulted in making this dream a reality.

After two years of study and consultation, Feliciano A. Sarli, the most experienced national pastor of the Disciples, was asked, in May, 1943, to visit the more important towns and cities in the northern part of the Province of Corrientes and in the eastern part of the National Territory of the Chaco to make a survey of the conditions and needs in that region. The report which Sr. Sarli made of his survey showed careful study and was highly commendable. He had evaluated the religious, educational, moral,

economic, and social needs as he had found them.
Early in September of the same year he made a
second trip to that region for further study of conditions, particularly in the area of Resistencia. As
a result of these studies, plans were completed and
Sr. Sarli was asked to move with his family to
Resistencia to establish Evangelical church work.
This he did in December, 1943. Sr. Sarli's wide
experience in church work had fitted him well for
this task. He had served in Buenos Aires as pastor
in the Saavedra, Villa Mitre, and B e l g r a n o
churches, respectively.

At the age of twelve years Sr. Sarli began attending Sunday school in the Belgrano church and was
baptized at the age of seventeen. Later he accepted
the call to the Christian ministry and entered the
Union Theological Seminary. In 1924 he graduated
from the Seminary and was ordained the same year
in the Belgrano church of the Disciples of Christ.
He began his work as an assistant minister in the
Colegiales church, and also taught in *Colegio* Ward
for the next eleven years, teaching classes in Bible
and Christian ethics. In 1926 he was married to
Srta. Clelia Porri and they have four children, one
daughter and three sons. Sr. Sarli became active
in interdenominational work and when the Argentine
Federation of Evangelical Youth was organized, he
was elected as a member of the executive committee.
He then served for five years as editor of *Elevación
(Elevation),* established in March, 1927, which was
the official publication of the interdenominational
youth organization. He is author of the book published in Spanish in Buenos Aires, 1943, entitled
Simiente en el Surco (Seed in the Furrow).

Resistencia had a population of 70,000 inhabitants and was a growing, progressive city in that section of the country. It was west of the Parana River and not far from Corrientes, a city which the Disciples Mission had considered entering some years previously. Writing at that earlier date, Robert B. Lemmon said the following:

"Up to Corrientes" does not sound very big, but up to Corrientes and return was just about fifteen hundred miles. For a Mission that is supposed to be taking care of these two great provinces . . . and another smaller one, we have a long way to go. The pity of it is that there are so many people there that need what we have to give them, but the consolation is that there are not one-tenth as many as there will be in less than fifty years. It is going to develop as our own great Mississippi Valley has developed. There are twenty-three cities where we ought to have preachers now, more than fifteen [cities] of them having more than ten thousand inhabitants. Two of these are state capitals, not much smaller than Lincoln, Nebraska.[2]

The characterization of this part of Argentina around Corrientes as presented by Mr. Lemmon has been well substantiated by the twenty-five years of development since the time he wrote.

Sr. Sarli immediately became active in his new field and was alert to the conditions and opportunities which faced him. He and his wife with their four children established themselves in the new community and won the friendship and confidence of a large number of people. As a result of these new contacts the work was officially opened in March, 1944. The Sunday school enrollment grew normally and by the middle of the year there was good attendance at both Sunday school and church services.

[2]*World Call*, Sept. 1919, p. 43.

Disciple churches in Buenos Aires took active interest in this new project and it rapidly became a center of Evangelical church work in that part of Argentina. Sr. Sarli, in a letter at the end of July, wrote:

> You cannot imagine what this field offers and what one might be able to do here. If there is no unforeseen misfortune, we will soon have a church established in Resistencia. We began here with four members, all members of my family. Later we had seven. This was increased to eight and on Easter Sunday it was raised to ten. . . . The prospects are excellent for our work here.[3]

This work, located about two-thirds of the distance from Buenos Aires to Asunción, Paraguay, proved a strategic and wise move. Sr. Sarli and his family deserve credit for the commendable work they did in getting this new station established. It was not long until other preaching points were started and became outposts from this central congregation in Resistencia.

In Buenos Aires a forward step was the dedication, on February 25, 1940, of the new building of the Villa Mitre congregation. This structure was made possible due to the sale of a property bought by the Mission some years previous and used first as a dwelling for a missionary family and later occupied for several years by the Women's Training School. Work in this section of the capital city had been started more than twenty years previously by the early missionaries but had grown slowly. This new building, neatly furnished, was a positive addition not only to the Disciples' work but to the Evangelical movement in the Republic. It served

---

[3]From an unpublished letter, written in 1944. Translated by J. D. Montgomery.

the immediate congregation and also contributed to a more adequate architecture among Evangelical churches.

Srta. Jorgelina Lozada became pastor of this congregation during the depression and gave constructive leadership for more than twenty years. Under her leadership this congregation conducted an effective kindergarten for the children of the church and the community. A modest clinic gave needed service to underprivileged families. The building also provided an apartment which served as a parsonage. Shortly after the dedication of the new building a lot adjoining the property was purchased. In 1938, along with four other delegates from Evangelical churches in the River Plate Republics, Srta. Lozada was a delegate at the World Missionary Conference held in Madras, India. After her return she wrote the book entitled *La India Tradicionalista y el Servicio Social (Traditional India and Social Service)*, published in Spanish in Buenos Aires, 1940.

A visit to the mission field by an executive secretary of the home board is always a welcome occasion. This was uniquely true when Miss Lela E. Taylor in company with her mother, Mrs. Nora Taylor, and Mrs. Henry Fishback arrived in Buenos Aires on March 18, 1937. Miss Taylor's trip was in connection with her work as executive secretary of Latin America for The United Christian Missionary Society. It was her second visit to South America, the first being in 1925 when she and Dr. Stephen J. Corey attended the Congress on Christian Work in Montevideo. The visit of Miss Taylor proved to be a helpful and constructive one. An executive secretary is a vital connecting link between the churches at home and the younger churches on the field. The inspiration, the counsel, as well as the administrative work of an executive secretary on such a visit help to maintain understanding and continuity of policy. Twelve years had elapsed between this and her previous visit, which is too long a period between the visits of board secretaries who have the responsibility of particular fields. So in recent years The United Christian Missionary Society has established the policy that an executive secretary of the Foreign Division should visit the field of the newer churches once every two or three years. This maintains more constructive relationship and gives effective guidance to missionaries as well as to national workers.

Due to ill health, Miss Taylor found it necessary to resign her position as executive secretary in 1939, and in 1941 Mae Yoho Ward was named as her successor. J. D. Montgomery served as ad-interim executive secretary while on furlough in 1940-41. Mrs. Ward came to this position well prepared and with a wide and rich experience. Training received at Bethany College and at Yale University gave her a broad scholastic foundation. Her work in religious education with The United Christian Missionary Society provided an opportunity for practical experience. Later during one term of service as a missionary in Argentina she came to know the people of Latin America at first hand as well as to learn their language. As executive secretary she is beloved and appreciated by both the missionaries and national workers in the fields under her administration. In recognition of her distinguished service at

home and abroad, Culver-Stockton College conferred
on her the degree of Doctor of Letters in June,
1954. Mrs. Ward made her first administrative
visit to Argentina in the capacity of executive secretary during the autumn of 1944.

In *Colegio* Ward three important developments
took place during this decade. At the beginning of
the 1936 session, two new features were added to
the American School division. One was the opening
of a girls' dormitory which made it possible for
girls outside of Buenos Aires to enroll either in the
American School division or in the Spanish-speaking Argentine division. The other feature was the
inauguration of the American Junior College, which
was unique in being the only English-speaking school
of college grade in all Spanish-speaking South
America. This enlargement of *Colegio* Ward curriculum enabled boys and girls to continue their
first two years of college work before returning to
the homeland for their last years of university study.
J. D. Montgomery was named as dean of the Junior
College. During its second year the Junior College
reached its highest enrollment of about twelve
students. After some five years, however, it was
discontinued owing to the fact that the majority of
high school graduates were leaving for the United
States to enter college. At the beginning of the 1937
school year an annex to the American School division was rented in the northern district of Buenos
Aires, known as Belgrano, where many American
families lived. The establishment of this annex
proved such a success that two years later the entire
American School division of *Colegio* Ward was
moved to this part of the city.

The Union Theological Seminary in Buenos Aires made significant progress during this decade. As early as 1930 a study had been made of the advisability of uniting the Seminary for young men and the Training School for young women. This plan, however, was delayed until 1942, when the two institutions were merged and administered under one board of managers. That same year the new building for the institution was started and the cornerstone laid. This new building, of dignified Tudor architecture, was dedicated on August 1, 1943. It marked a forward step in ministerial training, not only for the republics of the River Plate but also for all Spanish-speaking South America.

On the cornerstone of the building are engraved the words *Embajadores de Cristo* (Ambassadors of Christ). This motto challenges students as they enter the building. In addition, three dates are engraved on the stone: 1884, representing the founding, under Methodist and Waldensian auspices, of the first theological seminary in this region; 1922, the date of the opening of the Women's Training School; and 1942, the date of the laying of the cornerstone and the fusion of the two institutions mentioned above as founded in 1844 and 1922, respectively. The Disciples had cooperated in the Seminary since 1917, and were co-founders of the Women's Training School.

The Seminary is interdenominational, international, and coeducational. It is strategic in location and unique in Spanish-speaking South America both in its scholastic standing and in its cooperative program. Its purpose is to prepare young people, irrespective of denominational affiliation, for the ministry of Christian service. At the time of the dedication of the new building there were three religious bodies cooperating officially in the institution: the Methodists, the Disciples of Christ, and the Waldensians. Since that time, the Presbyterians, U.S.A., have become officially affiliated. B. Foster Stockwell of the Methodist Mission, director since 1926 of the Union Seminary, was the moving spirit in promoting the merger of the two institutions and in securing the new building.

The Disciples had a significant part in the dedication of the new Seminary building. At a special service a plaque was unveiled to the memory of Mrs. Ralph Latshaw, for many years the beloved president of the state organization of Disciple women in Missouri. For this reason the women of Disciple churches of that state raised funds for the construction of a unit in the new building of the Union Theological Seminary in Buenos Aires. The library of the new Seminary building was the unit designated as the gift of the Christian Women's Missionary Council of the State of Missouri. Persons who participated in the unveiling ceremony of the memorial plaque included Miss Margaret Lawrence, a Disciple missionary en route to China, Miss Zona Smith, the first director of the Women's Training School, and Mrs. J. D. Montgomery who interested the women in Missouri in this project.

This more adequate equipment increased the efficiency of the Union Theological Seminary, resulting in an enlarged enrollment of students. A revised curriculum raised the standards of ministerial training which provided a five-year course for those taking the regular degree from the Seminary. In the student body in 1943 seven nationalities were represented, and by chance the same number of denominations. There were nineteen men students and fifteen women. In 1955 the enrollment was seventy-seven, fifty-five men and twenty-two women, representing nine nationalities and ten denominations.

During his last two terms of service as professor at the Union Seminary, Mr. Montgomery contributed to the production of literature in the Spanish language and served on the committee on literature of the Confederation of Evangelical Churches. He is author of the booklet published in Buenos Aires in 1937 entitled *Mujeres del Antiguo Testamento (Women of the Old Testament)*. He supervised the translation and publication of the Spanish edition of the book by Dr. Julius A. Bewer, *The Literature of the Old Testament*. The Spanish edition was published in Buenos Aires in 1938 under the title *La Literatura del Antigua Testamento*. During this same period the Spanish edition of the *Abingdon Bible Commentary* was published in Buenos Aires, in which Mr. Montgomery collaborated. Sr. Eulalio Burgos, a Disciple pastor, was one of two translators of Dr. Bewer's book. He also translated some of the chapters of the *Abingdon Commentary* and shared in the editorial work of the manuscripts in Spanish.

The book by Dr. Alonzo W. Fortune, *The Fountain of Life,* was published in Spanish by the American Bible Society under the title, *La Fuente de Vida*. It was issued in Buenos Aires by the Union Book Store, *La Aurora,* in 1937.

Published under the auspices of the Union Theological Seminary, the quarterly, *El Predicador Evangélico (The Evangelical Preacher)*, first appeared in July, 1943. It was designed to deal with the work of the minister and matters related to the pastorate. This brought to fruition a long-felt need and has contributed constructively to the Evangelical ministry. Srs. Feliciano A. Sarli and Eulalio Burgos, Disciples, have both served as associate editors of this magazine.

In October, 1943, *River Plate Reflections* was first issued by the Disciple Mission in Buenos Aires. After the first numbers, this little magazine has been issued quarterly by the Disciples of Christ Paraguayan and Argentine Missions. It is published in Buenos Aires in the English language and is designed mainly for readers in the United States. It has served as a news magazine and is valuable for historical records.

Perhaps the most important step for two decades in the interest of cooperation among the Protestant churches in the River Plate Republics was taken on April 25, 1939, when the Confederation of Evangelical Churches was officially constituted. The previous year, at the annual meeting of the local Committee on Cooperation in Latin America, plans for a more representative organization were made the subject of special study. At another assembly on July 18, 1938, a provisional constitution was approved and the continuation committee was instructed to present it in revised form to the various church bodies, requesting that an official delegate be named for an assembly to be held in April, 1939.

In the constituting assembly twenty-five officially appointed delegates represented the following eight denominations: Methodist, Waldensian, Mennonite, Scots Presbyterian, Disciples of Christ, Evangelical Union of South America, Christian and Missionary Alliance, and the French Evangelical Church. The German Congregational Church was officially affiliated but without representation. Religious bodies and organizations sending fraternal delegates to the assembly were: Anglican, United Lutheran, Southern Baptist, Danish Lutheran, German Evangelical Church, Brethren Church (U.S.A.), Salvation Army, Y.W.C.A., Y.M.C.A., the American Bible Society, and *Colegio* Ward.

At this assembly the Confederation of the River Plate Republics (Argentina, Paraguay, Uruguay) was formally constituted and a constitution was adopted. An able and representative executive committee was elected to carry forward the work of the Confederation. Juan E. Gattinoni, bishop of the Methodist Church, was elected president. Emmanuel Galland, pastor of the French Evangelical Church in Buenos Aires, gave invaluable help in forming the new organization. He was devoted to the cause of cooperation among the Protestant churches and possessed keen administrative ability. The Disciples of Christ Central Council of Churches was represented by two official delegates, Srta. Jorgelina Lozada and J. D. Montgomery. In addition, another Disciple, Samuel S. McWilliams, was present as a fraternal delegate from *Colegio* Ward. The Disciples of Christ have had continuous representation on the executive committee of the Confederation and have been enthusiastic participants in the work of the organization. In 1944 Dr. Jorge Wenzel, a Disciple, was named executive secretary of the Confederation, giving half time to this work.

During this decade Evangelical Christians in Argentina, particularly in Buenos Aires, were blessed by visits of missionaries to other countries who were routed through Argentina because of the inconveniences of war travel. Within a period of some two years more than one hundred missionaries of various denominations passed through Buenos Aires, either on their way home or returning to the field. Mr. Montgomery, upon the request of The United Christian Missionary Society, had become the contact person in Buenos Aires for missionaries of his board. After a few Disciple missionaries traveled this way, many others followed. They found this route possible to reach Africa, Jerusalem, India, and even China. Some needed to stay over in Buenos Aires before transportation was available and their contact with the Evangelical churches was a source of inspiration and enrichment. Among the visitors in this group was Dr. P. D. Sukhnandan of the Disciple India Mission who spent a fortnight in Buenos Aires on his return to India in 1942, after studying in the United States. Writing in 1943 regarding these missionaries, Mr. Montgomery said:

> It is one of the noble testimonies of the Christian witness that during these days when there is so much aggression and destruction these men and women are willing to endure hardship and bear privation in the interest of goodwill, brotherhood, and Christian service.[4]

In this decade the Disciple outreach had established work in the city of Resistencia with a preach-

---

[4]From an unpublished article.

ing point in Barranqueras. This was strategic as it extended the work outside of the Capital City into the Province of El Chaco, taking the church work into a provincial capital. The number of missionaries on the field had again been raised from two couples, to which it had been reduced in the 1930's to three missionary couples and one single missionary. This showed results in outreach and growth, and led to the enlistment of more Argentine young people for Christian service.

In the cooperative work, in which the Disciples shared, growth and enlargement had also been a c h i e v e d. The Confederation of Evangelical Churches, which integrated more fully the cooperative work among the churches, had been organized, making the work more indigenous and effective. The interdenominational Pastors' Institute had grown to where its impact upon the Evangelical community was felt in a much larger way. The uniting of the Seminary for young men and the Training School for young women into the Union Theological Seminary and the dedication of the new buildings for the Seminary marked a forward step. These were important and far reaching. The new buildings gave to the Seminary a permanent location and equipment suited to its needs, both of which added to its efficiency and gave it standing among the Evangelical churches.

CHAPTER VIII

A Decade of Local Church Development
1946-1956

During this fifth decade of Disciple work in Argentina there were in evidence signs of continued growing pains of a vigorous and progressive republic. Progress within the country showed an increase in population and in internal development. In various areas industry grew stronger and agriculture maintained its vigor with larger exports to other countries. Significant in this period was the proposal by President Juan D. Perón in October, 1946, of the five-year plan of the government which was sanctioned by the National Congress. The broad scope of the plan included political, social, and economic projects which in part had already been undertaken, but were now to be combined into a program for long-range development. This plan included projects of public health, education, foreign service, social welfare, woman's suffrage, social security, housing, transportation, primary education and industrialization, foreign commerce and finance.

Progress in the field of education, art, literature, and journalism kept pace with that of government and of economic life. Argentina with one of the highest percentages of literacy of any American republic exceeded 86 per cent in 1951. In art and literature a high degree of attainment had been achieved. This was summarized by an observer as follows:

Buenos Aires has become in recent years one of the great publishing centers of America. In 1950, 262 newspapers were printed in the Argentine Republic, 1,267 periodicals, and 952 magazines and reviews. There are more than two hundred newspapers and periodicals printed in foreign languages. The volume of book-publishing is increasing rapidly.[1]

In the religious field trends were varied and marked. For more than fifty years previous to 1946 religious instruction was not permitted in government-supported public schools in the regular curriculum during school hours. (See Chapter II.) During this period a government decree which was enacted as a law in 1950 provided that teaching of the Roman Catholic religion should be given in all government-supported schools as well as all incorporated private schools, including the primary, secondary, and universities. Provision was made whereby the parents of Protestants, Jews, and other religious faiths could have their children exempt from this religious instruction upon formal request.

This new law provided that religious instruction in the schools would be under the Ministry of Education of the Federal Government with a representative of the Roman Catholic Church in its department. Religious instruction thus became a part of the curriculum in government-supported schools for almost a decade until its annulment at the end of 1954. Evidence available would indicate that political motives were involved. One weakness of the

[1]*Argentina* (Washington: Pan-American Union, 1952), p. 38.

system was the lack of teachers prepared to give the courses in religious instruction, which may have had something to do with its withdrawal.

During this same period a law was passed which required non-Roman Catholic religious bodies to register with the government. This provided accurate information regarding these religious bodies working in the country. Also it seemed to favor the dominant church and to limit the freedom of Evangelical groups. Apparently, however, this law did not dull the enthusiasm or curtail their activities.

The trend toward an emphasis upon religion within the Argentine culture which has been explained in previous chapters was of positive worth. It resulted in renewed interest in spiritual values as over against a materialistic philosophy. This showed gains both within the Roman Catholic Church and among Evangelical bodies. However, the close alliance between the Argentine government and the leaders of the dominant church resulted in the curtailment of the liberties of Evangelical churches. These restrictions were felt in many ways, among them the free use of communication through public channels.

The law of the country guarantees the freedom of religion. Yet in 1949 a new ruling was introduced which limited this guarantee of freedom. The new ruling explained that concerns of common interest may be violated by the full use of these freedoms. It was deemed wise to limit certain freedom if necessary in order to protect the common good. One area where full freedom was found not to be in the interest of all was that exercised by the press. News agencies were placed under surveillance of the government and in some cases dailies were taken over from private publishers.[2] This led also to restriction of certain activities on the part of non-Roman Catholic religious groups. An illustration of this was the restrictions placed on the use of the radio. A statement by Mae Yoho Ward written from Buenos Aires in 1951 shows how this operated:

> The report of the committee on Radio interested me greatly. Some years ago the Protestants had purchased radio time and broadcast every evening, for five minutes, evangelistic messages. Then the committee was notified that, since they had not properly registered with the government, broadcast would have to cease. It was found that all the necessary registration had been cared for, but still permission to broadcast was not given. In an effort to combat what appeared to be a violation of the freedom of speech, the Protestant forces obtained 25,000 signatures which were bound in the two volumes and sent to the President, with the request that they be allowed to broadcast. The matter was referred to the national office of radio broadcasting but up to date permission has not been granted. However, the Confederation continues work on the matter.[3]

Some of these restrictions were later lifted and the Protestant Churches were allowed time for radio broadcasting again during and following 1954.

Changes of Disciple missionary personnel during this decade, from 1946 to 1956, were varied and of more than usual importance. Thomas Jackson and Virginia Corrine Moore Liggett with their son, Thomas Milton, arrived in Argentina in 1946. He was from Florida and she from Kentucky. Their first two years of service were with the church at Resistencia, where their daughter, Margaret Ann,

---

[2]Among dailies judged to violate this freedom was the well-known daily in Buenos Aires, *La Prensa,* which was taken over by the government and the publisher, Dr. Alberto Gainza Paz, exiled from the country.

[3]*River Plate Reflections,* July, 1951, cover p. [1].

was born. They were then transferred to the Colegiales church in Buenos Aires for three years before going on furlough. Upon their return they were assigned to the Union Theological Seminary in Buenos Aires where they served as faculty members, representing the Disciples.

In March, 1946, Miss Rossie Elizabeth (Betty) McCaw was transferred from *Colegio Internacional,* Asunción, Paraguay, to the American School division of *Colegio* Ward in Buenos Aires. Born in Illinois, she spent the first three years of her life in the Philippines where her parents, Mr. and Mrs. Clayton C. McCaw, were missionaries. In December, 1946, she returned to the United States and was later married to John Johannaber, a Methodist. They have three children.

Drs. George Earle and Margaret Richards Owen with their two children, Mary Devon and Anne Franklin, returned to the States on furlough in 1948 after one term of service. Peggy, the third child, was born in 1949. Later they were transferred to the Philippine Mission and in 1955 to an executive position with the United Society in Indianapolis. Miss Hallie Lemon, after seven years in Buenos Aires, was transferred to the Disciple work in Asunción, Paraguay, in 1951. Carl R. Garnett, a native of Kentucky, arrived in Buenos Aires at the beginning of 1951 to serve as a contract teacher on the faculty of the American School division of *Colegio* Ward. When this division of the school was merged with the new American Community School, he returned to the United States.

Leonard Edward and Lucile Horner Vaughn reached Buenos Aires as new missionaries in May,

1954, and were assigned to the pastorate of the Villa Mitre Church. He was a native of Virginia and she was from Colorado. They have three small sons, Edward, James, and John.

Paul and Lucy Andress with their ten-year-old son, Robert, returned to the States on furlough in 1954. After a year in the States they were sent to Asunción, Paraguay, where Dr. Andress became director of *Colegio Internacional*. Mrs. Andress is author of the book published in Spanish in Buenos Aires in 1954 entitled *¿De Donde Vine, Mama?* *(Where Did I Come From, Mama?)*. It deals with sex education of the child from infancy to adolescence. The book is well illustrated, giving answers to questions which children so frequently ask during their early years. Mrs. Andress deals with these questions as a mother. The book is intended for use by parents in the home.

In February, 1955, William George and June Humphries Smedley, with their three children, Linda, Billy, and Bobby, were transferred from the Disciple Mission in Asunción, Paraguay, to *Colegio* Ward in Buenos Aires to replace Mr. and Mrs. Samuel S. McWilliams.

The transfer of missionaries from the Disciple Mission in Argentina to the Disciple Mission in Paraguay or vice versa has been practiced since the two Missions were founded. In the early years of the two Missions there was one administrative body with an annual meeting of missionaries and a continuing ad-interim advisory committee. This was discontinued in the early 1930's due largely to reduced budget. However, the common cultural background of the two countries, the common language, and the similar work of the two Missions make the transfer of missionary personnel convenient and mutually helpful.

Samuel S. and Alice Sheplee McWilliams occupy a place of distinction in being the first Disciple missionaries to round out their life service in Argentina. They retired from the field, after thirty-five years of service, in January, 1955. As a young couple, full of enthusiasm and with a broad vision, Mr. and Mrs. McWilliams arrived in Buenos Aires in 1919. With the exception of four years spent with the Disciple Mission in Mexico, they gave these thirty-five years to *Colegio* Ward. Perhaps no missionary couple ever worked more harmoniously as a team than did Samuel S. and Alice S. McWilliams. They loved and appreciated the Argentine people and they made many enduring friendships among them. Both were teachers in *Colegio* Ward. For many years Mr. McWilliams was vice-director and treasurer of the school, which place he filled with distinction. Mrs. McWilliams served many years as the capable secretary of the Board of Managers of the school. A Methodist colleague once said of Mr. McWilliams that he was doing one of the finest jobs in religious education at *Colegio* Ward that it had been his privilege to observe. Under the supervision of Mr. McWilliams a department of counseling and guidance was organized. Through this department *Colegio* Ward endeavors to guide and counsel its students through individual and group contacts so that they may make the best possible adjustment in school and home life and become happy, useful members of society.

The McWilliamses saw the enrollment in *Colegio* Ward grow from 160, with 32 boarding students, in 1920, to 800 students enrolled, with nearly 200 boarders, in 1954. They had seen the facilities of the school grow from a large old residence at Rivadavia 6100 in Buenos Aires, with limited playground, to modern and commodious buildings on a thirty-acre campus in the near-by suburb of Ramos Mejía. They had part in the observance of the fortieth anniversary of the school which was celebrated in 1953. Also, during these thirty-five years, they observed the growth of an expanding metropolis as stated below:

We have seen Buenos Aires grow from a million and a half population with one subway to 4,000,000 in Greater Buenos Aires, with five subways. But more than once when traveling on packed suburban trains or the underground, and when trying to push our way through the crowds on Florida Street in the late afternoon, we have longed for the more tranquil days of the smaller, less hurried city of the past.[4]

The efficient service and the congenial Christian influence of Mr. and Mrs. McWilliams extended far beyond the duties which *Colegio* Ward placed upon them. They participated in many activities of the Disciple churches and answered requests to speak in other pulpits as well as to participate in interdenominational activities. Although they had no children of their own, they were interested in Christian family life, and Mr. McWilliams became a popular speaker in Protestant churches and gatherings on this theme. The McWilliamses were much beloved by both the Argentine community and their fellow missionaries of all religious bodies.

[4]From an unpublished letter written Dec. 10, 1954.

Miss Zona Smith, veteran Disciple missionary to Argentina, passed away in Buenos Aires on December 22, 1952, at the age of seventy-eight. She is the only Disciple missionary to have been buried in Argentina. Many and varied were her contributions to the work of the Disciples as well as in the field of interdenominational endeavor.

She was one of the moving spirits in the founding in 1922 of the Women's Training School of which she was the first director. For twenty years she served on the Board of Managers of *Colegio* Ward and for the last ten years of her life was an honorary member. For many years she was general secretary of the Argentine League of Evangelical Women, founded in 1917, and for thirty-three years editor of its publication, *Guia del Hogar (Home Guide)*. Through that organization she projected her congenial personality and influence far beyond the walls of Disciple churches and even beyond the boundaries of Argentina to other Spanish-speaking countries. The love and esteem in which she was held by friends in her adopted land were shown in many ways. At her funeral on December 23, 1952, spoken words of appreciation bore testimony to her forty-two years of consecrated service to the cause of Christ in Argentina.

Eduardo Palaci, retired Lt. Colonel of the Salvation Army who had known Miss Smith for many years, said at the time of her death:

. . . Her life was similar to a diamond, cut with such art that its diverse facets reflected light and beauty in all directions. But, without doubt, the work that has engraved her name on the hearts of the Evangelical people of all Latin America was her work as editor of the magazine, *Guia del Hogar*. I do not think that there is any other Evangelical magazine dedicated to women that has been edited with more care, more zeal, and with more love and vision, than the one that for so many years has been edited by our beloved and unforgettable sister.[5]

An enriching experience for the Disciple work in Argentina was the sending of Frederick J. and Allene DeGaris Huegel to Buenos Aires from Mexico during three months of a furlough period in 1951. They made a contribution to both educational and evangelistic work, through classes at the Union Seminary, church services, interdenominational gatherings and the Pastors' Institute. Mr. Huegel, writing at the end of their visit, said:

> It was a great privilege to visit the Disciples here in Buenos Aires and to be able to preach the Word from the pulpits of their lovely Churches. One is struck by their beauty, especially Colegiales, which has all the charm of beautiful churches in the homeland. One is struck even more by the strength of those who come to worship and by the beauty and order of the services. The Easter Morning service will never be forgotten for it seemed as if a wave of joy and love swept through the congregation where I had given the Easter Message, sweeping everything before it. One saw men embracing and kissing each other on the cheek—it was indeed the holy kiss of which we read in the Word.[6]

The work of the Disciple churches during the ten years from 1946 to 1956 showed progress. At no time during the half-century was the membership of Disciple churches in Argentina large, but the number of members and their loyalty to the church had grown gradually. The report at the end of the missionary year 1954-55 showed that there were six churches, four in the city of Buenos Aires and two in the province of the Chaco, with a total member-

ship of 497. The ministry of Paul and Lucy Andress
as full-time pastors at the Colegiales church showed
constructive results. During the decade, 123 were
received into membership of the church. But more
significant were the gains in church organization
and in the educational program.

They led the church into a functional setup with
the following committees: evangelism and membership; stewardship and finance; Christian education;
dramatization; music and literature and publicity.
With these committees there developed a program
of training in churchmanship. The Christian Education Committee was well organized and the church
school was departmentalized with a two-hour ex-
panded session. Weekly offering envelopes were
introduced in the church services and the Sunday
morning service with communion became the important service of the week. The introduction of
religious drama added to the effectiveness of church
services at Christmas and Easter. Annual leadership training courses contributed to better-trained
leaders.

The work started in Resistencia in 1944 progressed normally and began to expand into near-by
communities. The most successful of these preaching points was in the town of Barranqueras in the
Province of the Chaco. It was there that Nicolás
Martinez established a Sunday school during his
year of practical studies as a student of the Union
Theological Seminary. This work grew and with
the help of The United Christian Missionary Society
and Disciple congregations in Buenos Aires a lot
with a small building was purchased in Barranqueras. Preaching services and Sunday school,

together with other activities for children and young people, were established.

In January, 1955, the congregation of Barranqueras was received into the Central Council of Disciple Churches in Argentina, and sent its first official lay delegate to the annual assembly and convention. This congregation has enthusiasm and initiative under the leadership of its pastor, Angel Peiró, as a report of its work early in 1955 shows:

One characteristic of the place in which the church is working is the inadequate housing—the majority of the homes being small structures of a single room in which live large families. The members of the congregation feel the need for helping each other to have better houses and already have worked together with two families. In one of these cases the pastor taught the people how to make large mud and straw bricks, a system unknown in this area, and much interest was shown. Within a little while another family will be helped to build its house using another economical method, which will serve at the same time as a demonstration to the neighbors to better their living quarters.[7]

A new venture was the work started in Tablada, an industrial suburb adjoining Buenos Aires on the southwest. This work was begun in 1950 as an outreach of the Villa Mitre church under the supervision of Srta. Jorgelina Lozada. After this work was established, it came under the administration of the Central Council of Churches and Eulalio Burgos was named as the first full-time pastor. He was followed in 1953 by Nicolás Martinez.

During this ten-year period two new Disciple church buildings were dedicated. One was the attractive structure for the Saavedra church in Buenos Aires. The procuring of this building is a normal story for the younger churches. Two lots

[7]*River Plate Reflections*, April, 1955, p. [5].

facing the open square in Saavedra were purchased
in 1931 and were used during some years as a playground for the youth of that congregation.   A
remodeled dwelling on an adjoining lot was used for
worship and church activities during the interven-
ing years.   In 1944 funds were available for a new
building, but increasing prices made it inadvisable
to build immediately.   Not until June 6, 1948, was
the cornerstone laid.   Prices continued to rise and
at times materials were scarce, causing delay in
construction.   Only the determination of the building committee and the patience of the constructor
kept things going until the building was finished.
Funds contributed by the Emergency Million for
Life and Work, supplemented by additional funds
from A Crusade for a Christian World, made it possible to complete the church and the pastor's apartment.   The building was dedicated October 8, 1950.

On Sunday evening, February 3, 1952, the lovely
new church building in Resistencia was dedicated.
The lot for the location of this new church, purchased in 1947, was made possible because of the
deep interest and the gifts of the Wilshire Boulevard
Christian Church of Los Angeles, California, and
the First Christian Church of Tyler, Texas.   The
grounds were ample for the church sanctuary, educational facilities, and a parsonage.   This provided
equipment for worship and space for Christian education and social service to the community.   The
cornerstone for this new building was laid on April
29, 1951.   Mrs. Mae Yoho Ward, executive secretary
for Latin America of The United Christian Missionary Society, who was on an official administrative

visit to Argentina, was present and had part in the ceremony.

The dedication of this building was one of interest and dramatic moment. Representatives of Disciple churches in Buenos Aires who had part were Silvio Azzati, president of the Disciple Central Council of Churches; Eulalio Burgos, pastor of the Saavedra church; Paul Andress, pastor of Colegiales; and Luis Mendizabal, layman of the Colegiales church and secretary of the Central Council.

The program of dedication began with the turning over of the keys of the new building by the constructor, Angel Peiró, to Paul Andress as representative of The United Christian Missionary Society. He in turn gave them to Silvio Azzati, president of the Council of Churches, who opened the door of the sanctuary and presented the keys to the pastor. Nicolás Martinez, pastor of the church, presided at the dignified service of worship that followed. The Scripture lesson was read by Federico Ruiz Díaz, member of the official board of the Resistencia church. The sermon was preached by Feliciano A. Sarli, who had begun the work in Resistencia eight years previously. The formal dedication was led by Paul Andress, and Silvio Azzati offered the dedicatory prayer.

This is the first Protestant church to be erected in Resistencia, the capital of the Province of the Chaco. The Disciples of Christ can well be proud of this pioneer work of the Protestant movement in Argentina. This building is another of the visible results of A Crusade for a Christian World.

An item of interest related to the construction of this new building was the personality of the architect

and constructor, Angel Peiró. He was a Disciple
student in the Union Theological Seminary in
Buenos Aires from the Colegiales church. The
planning and the supervision of the construction of
this building were done as a part of his year of
practical work, which the Union Seminary requires
of its students before their final year of studies. He
had prepared to be a builder and architect before
deciding to study for the ministry and this was a
demonstration of how he could use his technical
knowledge in the cause of the Kingdom.

Another interesting story connected with this
seminary student was his marriage almost a month
previous to the dedication, on January 10, in the
sanctuary of this church, the first ceremony of any
nature to be held there. His bride, Srta. Winnie
Elsie Morgan, was a member of the Resistencia congregation and also a student in the Union Seminary
preparing herself as a social worker. Sr. Peiró
and his bride were graduated from the Seminary
in November, 1952. The following January he was
ordained to the Christian ministry at the annual
convention of the Disciples of Christ held in Buenos
Aires and was named pastor of the congregation in
Barranqueras.

Perhaps no phase of the work of the Disciples of
Christ in Argentina during this decade, 1946-1956,
was more encouraging than was the number of
young people in preparation for Christian service.
Their interest and dedication was evidence that the
investment in the Union Theological Seminary was
paying dividends. In this ten-year period five Disciple students were graduated from the Union Seminary: Nicolás Martinez 1947, Srta. Magdalena

Gimena 1951, Angel Peiró 1952, Sra. Winnie E. Morgan de Peiró 1952, and Srta. Elvira Cestari 1953. Four of these students were of the Colegiales congregation and one from Resistencia. Other young people enrolled in the Seminary were: José Martinez de Castilla of the Villa Mitre church; Norberto Sarli, of the Saavedra church; Osvaldo Guiducchi and Srta. Emilia Gimena of the Colegiales church; Nancy Morgan and Juana Arregín of the Resistencia church; and Manuel Cuenca and Ramona Franco of the church in Asunción, Paraguay.

Srta. Magdalena Gimena was ordained to the ministry of Christian education in the Colegiales church on March 9, 1952. She worked as director of religious education of the Colegiales church until she went to the United States in 1953 on scholarship to continue her studies. While in the United States she studied at the University of Michigan and at Scarritt College and Vanderbilt University in Nashville, Tennessee. She had opportunity for practical experience by taking part in summer conferences and a laboratory training school for children's workers. On returning to Buenos Aires in 1954 she was again assigned to the Colegiales congregation as director of religious education. In January, 1955, she was put in charge of the work in Tablada, giving part time to the Belgrano church. On March 5 of that year she was married to Luis Parrilla, a ministerial student in his senior year at the Union Seminary.

Srta. Elvira Cestari from early childhood was a part of the Colegiales congregation. She is a third-generation Christian, her father and her grandfather having served as members of the Colegiales church board. At an early age her father died and with her mother and two sisters she continued in the Colegiales church where in her early teens she was baptized. After graduation from Normal School in Argentina she became a teacher in the week-day kindergarten in the Colegiales church, which position she continued part time for eight years. During this time she studied at the Union Theological Seminary and was the first Disciple woman to receive the Bachelor of Divinity degree in Argentina. Following her graduation she was transferred to Asunción, Paraguay, and in 1954 became a teacher in *Colegio Internacional*.

During this decade the Carnahan Lectureship was established in the Union Theological Seminary in Buenos Aires. The speakers for the first five years were: Dr. Harold A. Bosley 1951; Dr. W. A. Visser 't Hooft 1952; Dr. John A. Mackay 1953; Dr. Daniel T. Niles 1954, and Dr. John Baille 1955.

Capable lay members were increasingly taking places of responsibility in the work and leadership of the congregations. An indication of this development was the naming of a layman, José Miguel Font, in January, 1954, as treasurer of the Central Council of Disciple Churches, the first Argentinean to hold this position.

Other laymen who had continued for many years with the church did so in face of hardship because of their Evangelical faith. Dr. Eusebio D. Rodríguez and his brother José were baptized in the Belgrano church as young men in 1926. Rodríguez, who remained faithful to the church, met opposition in his own family because of his membership in a Protestant church. Later he wrote:

My religion and church meant everything to me; I found my companionship, my recreation, and my inspiration for life there. After the death of my mother, my father, who did not understand and was not in sympathy with the Protestant teachings, said to me one day that I could not continue living in his home if I insisted on going to the Protestant church. I had to make a choice, so I chose to stand by my convictions and left home at the age of twenty-one to live with my grandmother until I married a Christian girl and we established our own home. I have never regretted the choice I made to stand by the church and its teachings. It has shaped my whole life. In my work with the Argentine Department of Education, as a teacher and as an attorney, I have faced many similar choices, but have found joy and strength in following the teachings of my Master and guide, Jesus Christ.[8]

Dr. Eusebio D. Rodríguez became a teacher in the public schools and worked for a number of years in the Department of Education of the Argentine government. Later he received the degree of Doctor of Laws at the University of La Plata in the city of La Plata. In November, 1954, together with his wife and two daughters, he came to the United States and accepted a position in the state of New York. Dr. Rodríguez was named as a member of the executive committee of the World Convention of the Disciples of Christ in 1952 and with his family attended the World Convention in Toronto, Ontario, Canada, in 1955.

During this decade a new interest in sacred music was manifest among Disciples churches in Buenos Aires, particularly on the part of younger Christians. A choir, including members from the various churches, was organized which contributed to the

---

[8]From an unpublished statement by Dr. Eusebio D. Rodríguez, made in 1951. Translated by J. D. Montgomery.

devotional and spiritual life of the congregations and aroused new interest in the place of music in worship. Silvio A. Azzati was the director of this choir.

The first assembly of the women of the Disciple churches in Argentina was held in Buenos Aires on October 19-20, 1951. This assembly was organized by the women's committee of the Central Council of Churches. The main topics discussed during the three sessions were: "The Contribution of the Christian Family to the Life of the Church," "Christian Stewardship," "Health," and "Church Loyalty." This assembly became an annual function. In 1954 Srta. Jorgelina Lozada was elected as secretary of Argentine women's work among the Disciples, to which position she was to give half-time service.

During this decade, 1946-1956, there were four official administrative visits from the home office in Indianapolis. Mrs. Mae Yoho Ward visited the field in 1947 when she was accompanied by her fifteen-year-old son, Don Jeff, and again in 1951 when she made the trip alone. Dr. E. K. Higdon, executive secretary of the department of missionary selection and training of the United Society, in company with Mrs. Higdon, visited Argentina in 1949. In 1953, Dr. Virgil A. Sly, chairman of the Foreign Division of The United Christian Missionary Society and executive secretary for Africa and Japan missions, made a trip to Argentina as an exchange trip with Mrs. Ward who traveled to the Belgian Congo in 1954.

A significant publication for the Disciples was the Spanish edition of the book by Dr. Winfred E.

Garrison, *An American Religious Movement.* This was translated and published in Buenos Aires in 1950 under the title, *Los Discípulos de Cristo, una Breve Historia (The Disciples of Christ, a Brief History).* This is the most complete history of the Disciples of Christ that has been published in the Spanish language.

This decade showed the growing ecumenical phase of mission work as is illustrated by Argentine Disciples who were official delegates to conferences in the Americas and Europe. Dr. Jorge Wenzel, as executive secretary of the Confederation of Evangelical Churches, was a delegate to the second conference of the Latin American Union of Evangelical Youth in Havana, Cuba, August, 1946, the first conference having been held in Lima, Peru, in 1941. Following the conference in Havana, Dr. Wenzel came to the United States where he taught Spanish and did special study in Lynchburg College, Lynchburg, Virginia. His wife and daughter joined him there. Together with his family, he attended the World Convention of the Disciples of Christ in Buffalo, New York, in 1947. There Dr. Wenzel was elected one of the vice-presidents of the World Convention. He was the official representative of the Confederation of Evangelical Churches at the constituting assembly of the World Council of Churches in Amsterdam, Holland, in August, 1948. At the same assembly, Dr. B. Foster Stockwell and Dr. George Earle Owen were accredited visitors from Argentina for the Confederation. Dr. Wenzel was a delegate to the world convention of the World Council of Christian Education and Sunday School Association, held in Toronto, Ontario, Canada, in

1950, representing the Confederation of Evangelical Churches of the River Plate Republics.[9]

In 1947, Sr. Feliciano A. Sarli received a scholarship for academic study in the United States and was named by the Disciple churches of Argentina as their delegate to the World Convention of the Disciples of Christ, held in Buffalo, New York, in August, 1947. He studied at The College of the Bible, Lexington, Kentucky, during the summer of that year and participated in youth and adult conferences.

In March, 1950, Srta. Jorgelina Lozada spent some weeks in Geneva, Switzerland, working with the Commission on Women's Life and Work of the World Council of Churches. During the same year she attended the world convention of the World Council of Christian Education and Sunday School Association, held in Toronto, Ontario, Canada. In July, 1952, she attended the International Missionary Council's enlarged committee meeting at Willingen, Germany, where 200 delegates from fifty countries took part. She was a visitor at the second assembly of the World Council of Churches, in Evanston, Illinois, in August, 1954.[10] The program for the World Day of Prayer in 1955, sponsored by the United Church Women of the National Council of the Churches of Christ in the U. S. A., was prepared by Srta. Lozada.

[9]In the autumn of 1950, Dr. Wenzel accepted a position as professor at Ashland College, Ashland, Ohio. Later he went into business and settled at Ashland with his family. He has applied for citizenship in the United States.

[10]Both at the meeting of the International Missionary Council and the second assembly of the World Council of Churches, Srta. Lozada was chosen as a delegate or visitor by agencies of these bodies and the expenses of her travel were paid by them or from an interdenominational budget provided for this purpose. The same was true of other trips she made to ecumenical gatherings. The expenses of Dr. Jorge Wenzel for trips mentioned above were provided in a similar manner.

The spirit of cooperation among Evangelical youth during this decade was shown in the development of the Latin American Union of Evangelical Youth which was the result of their own initiative. The Union came about through a confederation of different area federations of Evangelical youth. Earlier in this book reference was made to the Argentine Federation of Evangelical Youth. It was one of a number of regional, interdenominational youth organizations throughout Latin America which joined to form the Latin American Union of Evangelical Youth. At a conference held in Lima, Peru, in 1941, the Union was established. At this conference there were thirty-nine delegates, representing eleven countries and eight denominations. The second conference was held in Havana, Cuba, in 1946, when there were sixty-five delegates, representing organizations in nine Latin American countries. The third conference met in Buenos Aires, in 1951, at which there were seventy-eight delegates representing fourteen countries. Disciples were among the representatives at all three conferences as Disciple youth have been active in this cooperative movement. At these conferences, in addition to the official delegates, there were also fraternal delegates and counselors in attendance.

The training of leaders is one of the most important tasks in the program of Christian education. But as important as this task is in the life of any church, the need for training lay leaders in the young churches on the mission field is even more acute than in the homeland, since the church does not have years of experience upon which to draw. However, in this decade, Disciples of Christ churches in Argentina made constructive progress. In part this was done in cooperation with other Protestant churches.

The first Laboratory Training School for vacation church school teachers, initiated by Dr. George Earle Owen, was held in the Colegiales church in 1945. Later this became an interdenominational enterprise and has been widely used in the training of church leaders.

The methods used in the laboratory school became effective in other types of training schools for lay leaders. One of these was the workshop where demonstration and practice features were used. In 1952 the Christian education committee of the Central Council of Churches, of which Srta. Magdalena Gimena was chairman, planned a series of workshops to be held in Disciple churches. In these workshops principles of teaching were demonstrated and worship services added devotional experiences.

The summer conference program, established in the River Plate Republics by the Y.M.C.A., offers another means for the training of lay leaders. The first interdenominational summer youth conference was held on the campus of *Colegio* Ward in 1927. This conference movement has continued annually with four conferences held in the summer of 1955, all planned by the Christian education committee of the Confederation of Evangelical Churches. These conferences were for intermediates, senior high, young people, and adult-family camp. There were in attendance at these conferences 179 persons, representing thirteen communions. As a part of this program special training was provided for leaders in the summer conference program.

An effort to develop an indigenous curriculum of Christian education in Latin America was initiated at a meeting of the World Council of Christian Education and Sunday School Association held in Mexico City in 1941. The study was continued at a Latin American Curriculum Conference held in Buenos Aires in 1949. Lenders at this conference included Dr. Forrest Knapp of the World Council on Christian Education from New York and Dr. G. Baez-Camargo, executive secretary of the literature committee of the Committee on Cooperation in Latin America, from Mexico City. This conference recommended a full-time executive secretary for the continuation of this work. The second Curriculum Conference met in Cienfuegos, Cuba, in May, 1950, when forty-five leaders from fourteen countries met to work on a new curriculum for Evangelical church schools in Latin America. Outlines prepared for the new curriculum were to be interdenominational and international in scope. The first units of this curriculum were published in 1954.

Increased attention was then given to the need of better-trained leaders. A Regional Conference was held in Santiago, Chile, in 1953 to develop a program of leadership education for Evangelical churches in various Latin American countries. Specific attention was given to three distinct groups: volunteer lay-workers, schoolteachers, and ministers. Four Disciple delegates from Argentina attended this conference: Paul Andress, Srta. Jorgelina Lozada, Srta. Magdalena Gimena, and T. J. Liggett.

The Confederation of Evangelical Churches enlarged its activities and the Disciples continued to

participate actively in its work. The annual report
of the Confederation presented in 1955 showed
twenty-two religious bodies as members and seven
affiliated institutions such as the Union Bookstore,
the Union Theological Seminary, etc. Twelve commissions planned extensive work for the Confederation. The commissions were: social action, help to
Spanish Christians, ecumenicity, Christian education, evangelism, youth, finances, literature, wom-
en's work, service to the press, radio, and public
relations. In 1951, Paul Andress served as secretary of the Commission on Christian Education,
giving one-third of his time to this phase of the
work. In 1954, Srta. Jorgelina Lozada was appointed to this office as half-time secretary.

A significant change took place in the history of
Colegio Ward in 1952. In July of that year the
American School division lost its identity with
Colegio Ward and, along with the other American
School in the city, became the new American Community School. Beginning some thirty years previously with the children of a few United States
parents living in Argentina, the American division
of *Colegio* Ward grew steadily until in 1952 its students numbered 400, 212 in grammar school and 188
in high school. About one-third were American
students, almost one-half Argentineans, and the rest
divided among thirty-five other nationalities. Is it
any wonder that each class roll sounded like the
roll call of the United Nations?

The leaders of *Colegio* Ward naturally were re-
luctant to release the American School division, but
they were convinced that the change was for the

best and offered a greater opportunity for the growth of American education in Argentina. The Spanish-speaking and the American divisions of *Colegio* Ward had been administered separately and at different locations due to the different nature of the programs. The Spanish-speaking division followed more closely the program of instruction of the Ministry of Education of the Argentine Government, while it was essential that the American division of the school be located within reasonable distance of the majority of the American community.

Religious trends in the Argentine Republic at mid-twentieth century appear to show a decline from the authoritarian control of the dominant church.[11] Indications of this decline were the number of students in the Evangelical seminaries, the number of books being sold by Evangelical bookstores, and the number of Bibles being distributed. Evidence of the yearnings of people for a sound and forthright interpretation and manifestation of religion in their lives and in their community was indicated by the evangelistic campaign of Theodore ("Tommy") Hicks in Buenos Aires in May, 1954.[12]

The large number of people who gathered to hear this evangelist was reported by the Buenos Aires newspapers to have reached 150,000. This took place in nominally Roman Catholic Argentina. As *The Christian Century* compared this campaign of

[11]Discussion of this trend as it relates to the Argentine Government is found at the close of Chapter II.

[12]Mr. Hicks, an American, was formerly a Baptist preacher, but now classifies himself as an independent. Once in the construction business, he was healed by faith from what he believed to be a mortal illness. He then devoted himself to evangelism.

Tommy Hicks with that of Billy Graham in London, an editorial stated:

> . . . this American evangelist has hit Buenos Aires harder than Billy Graham hit London. He has drawn larger crowds. He has gathered the signed cards of more ''converts.'' He has commanded more front-page newspaper attention. He has stirred up more controversy. And with it all, he has set a larger question mark over against the future of an important portion of the Evangelical world mission. It is high time to do some serious thinking about the phenomenon of Tommy Hicks.[13]

In his meetings, Mr. Hicks placed great stress upon faith healing.

During and following the campaign of Mr. Hicks the sale of Bibles in Argentina jumped so that the warehouses of the Bible Societies were sold out and additional supplies were rushed to Buenos Aires by air. The Protestant bookstores also had heavy sales during 1954.

In January, 1955, Mr. Hicks returned to Buenos Aires for another evangelistic campaign. After only three meetings, however, in one of the large stadiums, the federal police closed down the meetings, ostensibly to investigate the charge that Mr. Hicks was practicing medicine illegally. The real reason may have been to comply with the prohibition against large meetings because of political conditions.

As one comes to the close of this chapter which ends the record of a half century of Disciple history in Argentina, he feels a sense of gratitude for what has been accomplished. Yet he is aware of the many opportunities that have gone unfulfilled, and of the open doors which have not been entered. But

[13]*The Christian Century,* July 7, 1954, p. 814. Used by permission.

as he evaluates the possibilities that lie before the Protestant churches in the Argentine Republic, he is convinced that the doors are open for the future. Enduring foundations have been laid and much pioneer work has been done. Institutions have been established and congregations have been organized. The efficiency with which local congregations carry on their mission as revealed in this chapter is an indication as to the ways doors will open to the Evangelical church in the future if unfaltering faith, stewardship, and consecrated leadership characterize those who are ready to enter. May the Disciples of Christ be alert to this challenge of the open doors in Argentina.

Chapter IX

Protestants Look
to the Future

In a commencement address delivered in 1920 to the first group of missionaries who went out under The United Christian Missionary Society, the speaker declared that Latin America was one of the most difficult of all the fields where the Society had missionaries. As the reason for such a significant announcement, the speaker cited the presence in those countries of a great dominant church that had been at work there since the days of the Spanish colonies. He surmised that tree stumps would have to be pulled by the roots and dynamite would have to be used in order to prepare that most fertile field for the sowing of good seed.[1]

Missionaries who have labored in those countries, particularly the River Plate Republics, know from experience that rubbing shoulders with the leaders of the Roman Catholic Church does not make for easy going. Too, they are aware that in those early days Evangelical work in Latin America was considered to be on probation.

However, such is no longer the case. Evangelical missions have passed the probationary stage and are on the march. In the great strategic centers of Latin America, Evangelical schools have been established and are hard at work presenting the Chris-

[1]Adapted from an address by Fred W. Hughes, delivered to the International Convention of Disciples of Christ in Miami, Fla., in 1954.

tian way of life to thousands of Latin American youth. There is scarcely a city of any size in South America that does not have such an institution.

A more significant contribution, however, which mission boards have made and are making in those countries is the development of Evangelical churches in which the gospel of our Lord and Savior is being preached every Lord's Day. In Argentina where Protestant work was established more than one hundred and thirty years ago, and where preaching in the Spanish language was permitted some forty years later, strong and vigorous Evangelical churches with good equipment and capable leadership work and worship. These Evangelical bodies grew and developed so that by 1950 there were in the city of Buenos Aires more than two hundred Evangelical churches and preaching points. One body alone, the Assembly of God, completed a church building in Buenos Aires in 1953 with a seating capacity of over 2,000. Evangelical churches have developed and are working in cities and towns throughout the republic. The census of 1947 in Argentina showed only two per cent of the population to be Protestants. Yet, Argentine Protestantism for many years has been a strong and growing force. The rate of increase of adherents to Evangelical churches has been more rapid than the rate of increase for the population as a whole. For instance, since 1895 the population of Argentina has quadrupled, while during the same period membership in Evangelical churches has increased twelvefold. Protestantism has taken root in Argentine soil.[2]

---

[2]See article by Thomas S. Goslin, *River Plate Reflections*, July, 1953, pp. [1ff.].

In addition to seminaries, schools, young people's societies, interdenominational women's organizations, Protestants carry on publishing enterprises, clinics, orphanages, homes for the aged, and related activities. The Union Bookstore, carried on jointly by a number of the Protestant bodies working in Argentina, is a busy establishment which sells thousands of Protestant religious books each month. Also, there is a Protestant bookstore conducted by the Southern Baptist Convention in Argentina.

The Argentine Constitution guarantees freedom of religion, which is a tremendous benefit to a dynamic, growing minority. The future of Protestantism in Argentina at the mid-century appears encouraging and the outlook is optimistic, in spite of political and economic conditions which seem to handicap it. There are perhaps ten times as many Argentine pastors and workers of the Evangelical churches as there are missionaries. Argentine churches are supplying more and more of their own leadership and financial support, leaving to the missionary the various specialized tasks for which he is particularly qualified; for instance, the opening of new work, leadership training, some phases of administration, and some areas of teaching.

As the Disciples of Christ close a half-century in the River Plate Republics they do so with humility because of opportunities unfulfilled and with justified satisfaction because of achievements realized. They take pride in having shared in the struggles and victories of the larger Evangelical movement for this half-century. During this period, perhaps the Disciples have placed major emphasis on the founding and the development of institutions of learning and on the laying of firm foundations for cooperative enterprises. The results have been constructive, presenting an entering wedge for a more direct evangelistic approach, and laying a basis on which to build a strong indigenous church.

The future concern of Protestants in Argentina should be the building of strong and effective Evangelical churches. Schools and institutions of learning could, in the future, easily pass out of the hands of church leaders and come under the control of the state which is responsible for the education of the people. In like manner the number of missionaries entering the country might be drastically limited. On the other hand a strong, indigenous church, with capable, well-prepared national leaders, has its roots much deeper in the soil of the country and so becomes more permanent and enduring.

May the Disciples of Christ share the appeal of this future concern of establishing more and stronger Evangelical churches in Argentina. May they share in telling the story of the Master and in building his Kingdom in a country in which it is estimated that three out of four people have no real religious allegiance. May they continue to be a part of that larger group who share the belief that a dedicated Protestantism, with the open Bible and the living Christ, has done much and in the providence of God will increasingly do more to bring Argentine friends into a saving knowledge of him who said, "I came that they may have life, and have it abundantly."[3]

---

[3]John 10:10b, Revised Standard Version.

Appendixes

1. LIST OF MISSIONARIES TO ARGENTINA

Name of Missionary	Date of Service	Total Years
Willis J. Burner	1905-1912	7
Mrs. Lulu Burr Burner	1905-1912	7
Edwin Wyle	1907-1909	2
Mrs. Alice Louise Wyle	1907-1909	2
Mrs. Maria Reynolds Ford	1910-1914	4
Miss Zona Smith[1]	1910-1933	23
Dr. Tolbert F. Reavis	1912-1925	13
Mrs. Mabel Yokley Reavis	1912-1925	13
Dr. C. Manly Morton	1916-1918	2
Mrs. Selah Louise Beam Morton	1916-1918	2
Robert B. Lemmon	1917-1924	7
Mrs. Mary Hilton Lemmon	1917-1924	7
Miss Mary Irene Orvis	1918-1923	5
Samuel S. McWilliams[2]	1919-1955	30
Mrs. Alice Sheplee McWilliams	1919-1955	30
Fred W. Hughes	1920-1921	1
Mrs. Mary Ingle Hughes	1920-1921	1

[1]Miss Smith continued in interdenominational work in Argentina an additional nineteen years, from 1933 until her death in 1952.

[2]The service of Mr. and Mrs. McWilliams included a four-year term in Mexico, 1926-1930.

Dr. Charles A. Vannoy	1920-1924	4
Mrs. Mary Adelaide Vannoy	1920-1924	4
Miss Ruth Ella Fish	1922-1931	9
Abner Johnson	1922-1925	3
Mrs. Olive Adamson Johnson	1922-1925	3
Howard T. Holroyd	1923-1930	7
Mrs. Leona McMahon Holroyd	1923-1930	7
Mrs. Lora Garrett Mehlis	1925-1931	6
J. Dexter Montgomery	1926-1944	18
Mrs. Anna Kate Givens Montgomery	1926-1944	18
Dr. Hugh J. Williams	1928-1931	3
Mrs. Winifried Williams Williams	1928-1931	3
Normal B. Ward	1928-1934	6
Dr. Mae Yoho Ward	1928-1934	6
Miss Ina L. Foster	1931-1933	2
Dr. Roy Paul Andress	1943-1954	12
Mrs. Lucy Wade Andress	1943-1954	12
Dr. George Earle Owen	1943-1948	5
Dr. Margaret Richards Owen	1943-1948	5
Miss Hallie Lemon	1943-1951	8
Thomas Jackson Liggett, Jr.	1946-	
Mrs. Virginia Moore Liggett	1946-	
Mrs. Rossie Elizabeth (Betty) McCaw Johannaber	1946-1947	1
Leonard Edward Vaughn	1954-	
Mrs. Lucile Horner Vaughn	1954-	
William George Smedley	1955-	
Mrs. June Humphries Smedley	1955-	

2. Concerning Argentine National Workers

(Listed approximately in the order in which they entered
the work)

Manuel Andrade and his wife were the first converts to
the Disciple work in Argentina. They were baptized
on June 26, 1907.

Sra. Emilia Echuariz, a widow, was baptized by Mr.
Reavis in 1912 during his first year in Argentina. She
served as a lay worker. She and her two sons helped
to open the work in La Paternal (now Villa Mitre)
in 1918.

Fernando Salem, Uruguayan, served as an Argentine national pastor for several years.

Manuel Blanco, an Argentinean, was baptized by Mr.
Reavis in 1912 during his first year in Argentina. He
served as a minister for some years.

Ramón García from Spain preached a number of years for
the Plymouth Brethren before becoming a minister
of the Disciples. He gave valuable help to Miss Zona
Smith in the translation of Peter Ainslie's book *God
and Me* into the Spanish language.

Blas A. Maradei, an Italian, was minister with the Disciples for a number of years, having formerly been
with the Southern Baptists.

Antonio de Césare, an Italian, attended the Union Seminary in 1918 and later came to the U.S.A.

Federico de Luque, a Spaniard by birth, attended the
Union Seminary and was a faithful helper in the Mission program. Later he became an architect and he
and his son, a constructor, built the present Villa
Mitre church building.

Rafael Galizia, an Argentinean, graduated from the Union
Seminary and served as a pastor for several years.
He also taught in the Women's Training School, *Cole-
gio Internacional* in Asunción, Paraguay, and in
Colegio Ward in Buenos Aires. He married Srta.
Emma Scardino, a nurse; they have one son.

Ambrosio Muñiz, a native Spaniard, attended the Union Seminary and was pastor of Disciple churches, serving in Villa Mitre, Saavedra, and Belgrano.

Silvio Azzati, an Argentinean and son of a pioneer Methodist minister, was graduated from Union Seminary in 1924, taught in *Colegio* Ward, and has served long pastorates in Colegiales and Belgrano. He married Srta. Elena Colmegna and they have a family of four children.

Feliciano A. Sarli, an Argentinean, was graduated from the Union Seminary in 1924. He is an ordained minister, an editor and writer, has been a pastor for more than thirty years. He taught in *Colegio* Ward, opened the mission station at Resistencia in the Province of El Chaco of northern Argentina and has been a leader in the interdenominational youth program. He married Srta. Clelia Porri and they have four children. He attended the World Convention of the Disciples of Christ in Buffalo, New York, in 1947.

Sra. Italina Azzati Riba, an Argentinean, was one of the first three graduates of the Women's Training School.

Srta. Jorgelina Lozada, an Argentinean, was graduated from the Women's Training School in 1925. She is an ordained Argentine minister, served the Villa Mitre church as pastor for more than twenty years, and has been active in the Confederation of Evangelical Churches in the River Plate. She has attended ecumenical gatherings in India, Europe, and in both North and South America. She prepared the 1955 World Day of Prayer program.

Sra. Aida Fernández Lozada, an Argentinean, graduated from the Women's Training School and served the women and children of the churches. She is now married to Jorge Lozada and is the mother of three children.

Sra. Julia Berro Marchi, an Argentinean, graduated from the Women's Training School and served the women and children in the church program.

Antonio García, a Spaniard by birth, was pastor of a Disciple congregation for seven years, 1938 to 1945.

Eulalio Burgos, Paraguayan by birth and trained in the Union Seminary, is an ordained minister and has served several pastorates in Buenos Aires and Resistencia. He has made a valuable contribution to Evangelical literature as a translator. He married Srta. Nelida Procher, who studied in the Women's Training School. They have two children. In 1955 he became a member of the staff of *Colegio* Ward.

Nicolás Martínez, an Argentinean, graduated from the Union Seminary in 1947 and is an ordained minister. During his first pastorate in Resistencia the new church building was erected. After one year with the Disciple work at Tablada in Buenos Aires he returned to the pastorate of the Resistencia church in 1955. He married Srta. Blanca Staude and they have three children.

Sra. Magdalena Gimena Parrilla is an Argentinean, a graduate of the Union Seminary in 1951 and an ordained Christian worker. She has served as director of religious education in the Colegiales church, in Belgrano, and in Tablada. She studied in the United States in 1953-1954.

Srta. Elvira Cestari, an Argentinean, is a graduate of the Union Seminary in 1953 with special training in kindergarten work. She served as kindergarten teacher and Sunday school worker in the Colegiales church and later became a teacher in *Colegio Internacional* in Asunción, Paraguay.

Angel Vicente Peiró, an Argentinean, was graduated from the Union Seminary in 1952 and became pastor of the Barranqueras church in northern Argentina. Before preparing for the ministry he was an architect and

built the Resistencia and Barranqueras churches. He
married Srta. Winnie Elsie Morgan, who also is a
graduate of the Union Seminary. They have two
children.

3. HIGH LIGHTS OF THE ARGENTINE MISSION

1905—Mr. and Mrs. W. J. Burner went out under the
Christian Woman's Board of Missions as the first
Disciple missionaries to Argentina.

1906—First sermon preached on Sunday, December 9, by
Mr. Airth at Olazábal and O'Higgins Streets in Belgrano, Buenos Aires.

1907—First convert baptized by Edwin Wyle on July 27.
—Disciples first celebrated the Lord's Supper, using
the Spanish language, on August 25.

1910—Preaching started in Colegiales on March 12.

1911—Belgrano church building (gift of Ohio Disciples)
on Cramer Street dedicated on January 22.

1914—First Christian Endeavor Society organized, in the
Belgrano church of Buenos Aires.
—Dr. Samuel Guy Inman, Disciple missionary to
Mexico, and later executive secretary of the Com-
tee on Cooperation in Latin America, visited Disciple work in Argentina at the request of the Christian Woman's Board of Missions.

1917—Cooperation begun with Methodists in *Colegio Americano.*
—Argentine League of Evangelical Women (interdenominational) founded. Its *Boletin* established that
year later became *Guia del Hogar (Home Guide).*
—Work in La Paternal (now Villa Mitre) started.

1918—Cooperation with Methodists in Union Theological
Seminary begun.
—Lots purchased for church building in Colegiales.
—Paraguay Mission of Disciples established in Asun-
ción with transfer of Mr. and Mrs. C. Manly Mor-
ton from Argentina.

1919—Work started in Saavedra, section of Buenos Aires.

1921—Mrs. Anna R. Atwater, first vice-president and secretary of Latin American missions of The United Christian Missionary Society, visited Argentina.

1922—Training School for Christian Women Workers founded in Buenos Aires by Disciples and Methodists.

1923—First Disciples graduated from Union Seminary, Buenos Aires.

1925—Dr. Stephen J. Corey and Miss Lela E. Taylor, missionary executives of The United Christian Missionary Society, visited Argentina.

—First graduation of Women's Training School, Buenos Aires.

1926—Land for *Colegio Americano* purchased in Ramos Mejía of Buenos Aires.

—*La Aurora* (Union Book store) established in Buenos Aires.

1927—First Young People's Conference (interdenominational) held at Ramos Mejía, Buenos Aires.

1928—Waldensians affiliated with Union Seminary.

1929—Argentine Central Council of Disciples Churches organized.

1931—Colegiales church, Buenos Aires, dedicated on March 15.

—Lots purchased in Saavedra for church building.

1932—Name of *Colegio Americano* changed to *Colegio* Ward.

—Three new buildings for *Colegio* Ward built at Ramos Mejía, Buenos Aires.

1933—Spanish-speaking division of *Colegio* Ward moved to Ramos Mejía.

1937—Celebration of thirty years of Disciple work in River Plate area.

—Miss Lela E. Taylor, executive secretary of Latin American missions of The United Christian Missionary Society, visited Argentina.

1938—Silver jubilee celebration of *Colegio* Ward.

—Belgrano division (American School) of *Colegio* Ward opened.

1939—Confederation of Evangelical Churches of River Plate Republics organized.

1940—Villa Mitre church, Buenos Aires, dedicated on February 25.

1941—First Conference of the Latin American Union of Evangelical Youth held in Lima, Peru.

1942—Union Seminary and Women's Training School merged on April 27.

—Silver anniversary of Argentine League of Evangelical Women observed.

—Rividavia Street property of *Colegio* Ward sold.

1943—Additional land in Ramos Mejía added to *Colegio* Ward campus in Buenos Aires.

—Union Seminary building dedicated.

1944—Resistencia church in the Province of El Chaco launched April 23 with eighteen members under the leadership of the Feliciano A. Sarli family, transferred to this work in December of the previous year.

—Mrs. Mae Yoho Ward, executive secretary of Latin American missions of The United Christian Missionary Society, made first administrative visit to Argentina.

1945—First Laboratory Training School for vacation church school teachers held in Colegiales church, Buenos Aires.

—Interdenominational English-speaking S u n d a y School organized in Belgrano, Buenos Aires.

1946—Second Conference of the Latin American Union of Evangelical Youth held in Havana, Cuba.

—Land for new church purchased in Resistencia, the Chaco Province.

—New dormitory constructed on *Colegio* Ward campus.

1947—Disciples and Methodists celebrate thirty years of cooperation in *Colegio* Ward.

—Presbyterians, U.S.A., affiliated with Union Seminary.

—Property purchased in Barranqueras, the Chaco Province.

—New church building in Saavedra begun.

—Mrs. Mae Yoho Ward, United Society executive, visited Argentina.

1948—Laboratory schools organized by Confederation of Evangelical Churches.

1949—Latin American Curriculum Conference held at *Colegio* Ward in Buenos Aires.

—Inter-American Evangelical Conference held at Union Seminary, Buenos Aires.

—Dr. E. K. Higdon, executive secretary of missionary selection and training for The United Christian Missionary Society, with Mrs. Higdon, visited Argentina.

1950—*Colegio* Ward dedicated Manual Arts building and Gymnasium-Auditorium.

—Committee on Study of Christian Education Curriculum met at Cienfuegos, Cuba.

—Saavedra church dedicated on October 8.

—Expansion work initiated in the industrial district of Tablada, Buenos Aires.

1951—Mr. and Mrs. F. J. Huegel, missionaries in Mexico, spent three months in Argentina.

—Mrs. Mae Yoho Ward, United Society executive, visited Argentina.

—Cornerstone of Resistencia church laid on April 29.

—First Congress of Disciple Women held in Buenos Aires.

—Third Conference of the Union of Evangelical Youth held in Buenos Aires.

—Lots in Tablada, Buenos Aires, bought for church building.

1952—Resistencia church dedicated on February 3.

—American School division of *Colegio* Ward merged with Lincoln School to form new American Community School.

1953—Evangelical Conference on Leadership Education held in Santiago, Chile.

—Union Seminary made recipient of Lopez Library (700 volumes) of Spanish Religious Literature.

—Dr. Virgil A. Sly, chairman of the Foreign Missions Division of The United Christian Missionary Society, made administrative visit to Argentina.

1954—New lots purchased for church building in Barranqueras, El Chaco Province.

—Union Seminary bought property for expansion.

1955—Dr. E. J. Bauman, alumnus, becomes first Argentine director of *Colegio* Ward on April 14.

—Williams Hall on *Colegio* Ward campus dedicated on April 14.

1956—Fiftieth anniversary celebration of the Argentine Mission of Disciples of Christ held in April.

Bibliography

BOOKS

Arciniegas, Germán, *The State of Latin America.* New York: Alfred A. Knopf, 1952.

Browning, Webster E., *The River Plate Republics.* London: World Dominion Press, 1928.

Burner, Willis J., *South America—Our Mission in Argentina.* Indianapolis: Christian Woman's Board of Missions, 1912.

Corey, Stephen J., *Among South American Friends.* Cincinnati: Powell and White, 1925.

— —. *Fifty Years of Attack and Controversy.* St. Louis: The Bethany Press, 1953.

Edmeston, Rhoda C., *The Protestant Youth Movement in Latin America.* New York: Committee on Cooperation in Latin America, 1954.

Elliott, Arthur E., *Paraguay, Its Cultural Heritage, Social Conditions and Educational Problems.* New York: Columbia University, 1931.

Harrison, Ida Withers, *History of the Christian Woman's Board of Missions.* Indianapolis: Christian Woman's Board of Missions, 1920.

Howard, George P., *Religious Liberty in Latin America.* Philadelphia: Westminster Press, 1944.

— —. *We Americans: North and South.* New York: Friendship Press, 1951.

Inman, Samuel Guy, "Argentina," *The Encyclopedia Americana.* 30 vols.; New York: Americana Corporation, 1953.

— —. *Latin America, Its Place in World Life.* New York: Willett, Clark & Company, 1937.

Irelan, Elma C., *Fifty Years with Our Mexican Neighbors.* St. Louis: The Bethany Press, 1944.

Latourette, Kenneth S., *A History of Christianity.* New York: Harper & Brothers, 1953.

Mackay, John A., *The Other Spanish Christ.* New York: Macmillan Co., 1933.

Morton, C. Manly, *Kingdom Building in Puerto Rico.* Indianapolis: The United Christian Missionary Society, 1949.

Panama Congress 1916, *Christian Work in Latin America.* 3 vols.; New York: Missionary Education Movement, 1917.

Pan-American Union, *Argentina.* Washington, D. C., 1952.

Perón, Eva, *My Mission in Life.* New York: Vantage Press, 1953.

Rennie, Ysabel, *The Argentine Republic.* New York: Macmillan Co., 1945.

Rojas, Ricardo, *The Invisible Christ.* New York: Abingdon Press, 1931.

Shaull, M. Richard, *Encounter With Revolution.* New York: Association Press, 1955.

Terán, Juan B., *El Nacimiento de la América Española.* Tucumán, Argentina: Miguel Violetto y Compañía, 1927.

— —. *La Salud de la América Española.* Paris: Casa Editorial Franco-Ibero-Americana, 1926.

The World Almanac 1955 and Book of Facts. New York: New York World-Telegram and The Sun, 1955.

They Went to Latin America. Indianapolis: The United Christian Missionary Society, 1947.

Ward, Mae Yoho, *Christian Action in Argentina.* Indianpolis: The United Christian Missionary Society, 1948.

— —. *Disciples of Christ in Latin American and Jamaica.* Indianapolis: The United Christian Missionary Society, 1951.

PERIODICALS

El Mensajero, Buenos Aires.
Guía del Hogar, Buenos Aires.
Missionary Tidings, Indianapolis.
River Plate Reflections, Buenos Aires.
The Christian Century, Chicago.
The Christian-Evangelist, St. Louis.
U. S. News & World Report, Washington.
World Call, Indianapolis.

UNPUBLISHED MATERIAL

Aden, Fred, Annual Report of *Colegio* Ward, 1933.
Azzati, Sra. Elena Colmegna, An Article, 1954.
Browning, Webster E., A Report, 1934.
Hughes, Fred, An Address, 1954.
Lozada, Srta. Jorgelina, A Personal Statement, 1954.
McWilliams, Mr. and Mrs. S. S., A Letter, 1954.
Montgomery, J. Dexter, A Statement, 1947.
— —. An Article, 1943.
Rodríguez, Dr. Eusebío D., A Statement, 1954.
Sarli, Feliciano A., A Letter, 1944.
Smith, Zona, An Address, 1927.
— —. An Article, 1911.

Index